More Killing Defence
at Bridge

HUGH KELSEY

London
VICTOR GOLLANCZ
in association with
PETER CRAWLEY

First published in 1972
by Faber & Faber Ltd

This edition first published 1993
in association with Peter Crawley
by Victor Gollancz, an imprint of Cassell,
Villiers House, 41/47 Strand, London WC2N 5JE

A catalogue record for this book
is available from the British Library

ISBN 0 575 04941 3

Printed in Great Britain by
St Edmundsbury Press Ltd, Bury St Edmunds, Suffolk

ACKNOWLEDGEMENTS

Once again I owe a debt of gratitude to my faithful proof-readers, Denis Young and Tom Culbertson. If this book is reasonably free from error it is due in no small measure to their diligent and ruthless application of the blue pencil.

H.W.K.

Contents

Introduction

My first bridge book, *Killing Defence at Bridge*, seemed to strike an immediate chord with readers and has gone on to sell more than 100,000 copies worldwide. I soon realised, however, that I had left a great deal unsaid on the subject of defence. This book, *More Killing Defence*, was my attempt to fill a few more of the gaps. It concentrates mainly on two important and neglected areas—the hazards of discarding and the control of options.

Although the welcome trend towards improved standards of play continues to accelerate, defence remains the weak spot for ninety-nine players out of a hundred. The truth is that defence is difficult. The defender constantly finds himself on unfamiliar ground, where technique is of little help and success can be earned only by the application of clear and logical thinking. The problems in this book are designed to guide the reader's thinking along the right lines. The quiz format has again been adopted, with only two hands shown at the top of the page so as to reproduce battle conditions as far as possible. To obtain the maximum benefit from a study of the book, the reader should make a serious attempt to work out the answer to each problem before going on to read the analysis.

1 • Bread and Butter Discards

Hundreds of volumes have been devoted to the play of the cards at bridge, and yet the most diligent search for advice about discarding is likely to end in disappointment. The subject is hardly mentioned in the text-books. It seems strange that bridge writers should take discarding so much for granted, since it is not only a highly skilled art but also a particularly vital one. Without some measure of mastery of this art, no player can hope to become a competent defender. Just think of the number of times you have been allowed to make an impossible contract owing to a careless discard by a defender. For that matter think of the defences you yourself have ruined by unguarding a critical suit at the wrong time.

Discarding is a common enough procedure. We have to find a discard or two on almost every hand we play, for a declarer does not have to be particularly skilful to see the advantages of playing out his long suit. Occasionally it will not matter how we discard, but in most cases it will matter very much. Apart from the obvious situations where a poor discard establishes an immediate or eventual winner for the declarer, faulty discarding can lead to all kinds of problems in the later play. The foundations of correct end-play defence are laid in the early stages by sound discarding, which therefore calls for a high degree of forethought.

In this chapter we are concerned with straightforward situations where the defender is not under any great pressure but where a careless discard may nevertheless prove fatal to the defence. The basic defensive skills of counting and inference will help to produce the right answer.

Love all
Dealer North
N   S
1 NT   4 ♠

♠ 8 6
♡ J 8 6 5
◇ A Q 7 3
♣ A K 5

♠ 2
♡ K Q 10 9
◇ J 10 8 5 2
♣ Q 8 4

West begins with the ace and another heart, your nine winning the second trick when dummy plays low. Declarer ruffs the third round of hearts and cashes the ace and king of spades, partner following with the five and seven while you discard the two of diamonds. The knave of spades is then led to West's queen, the five of clubs being discarded from dummy. What do you discard on this trick?

Obviously you cannot spare the heart, and at first glance a discard from either minor suit seems potentially dangerous. A count of declarer's tricks will keep you on the right track, however. If South started with seven spades, as seems likely, he will always come to ten tricks with the aid of the diamond finesse—unless he is void in diamonds. You can therefore afford to throw another diamond and keep your queen of clubs guarded.

Even if the declarer has only six spades, a second diamond discard from your hand cannot affect the issue. Partner's next lead will be a club, and South will be unable to make ten tricks unless he has the king of diamonds.

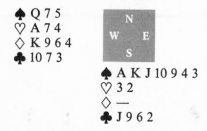

♠ Q 7 5
♡ A 7 4
◇ K 9 6 4
♣ 10 7 3

♠ A K J 10 9 4 3
♡ 3 2
◇ —
♣ J 9 6 2

```
              ♠ K Q 9 4 3
              ♡ A 9
              ◇ Q 9 3          N–S game
              ♣ Q 6 2          Dealer West
♠ A 10 8 2         N         W    N    E    S
♡ K 7 5 3                    1 ♠   —    —   1 NT
◇ A 10 4     W        E      —         3 NT  All pass
♣ K 7             S
```

You try a lead of the three of hearts against the three no trump contract. The nine is played from dummy, East puts in the ten and South wins with the queen. You play low on the lead of the five of spades and East drops the knave under dummy's queen. When the three of diamonds is led to South's knave, you take your ace and return the five of hearts to knock out the ace, East playing the two and South the four. The queen of diamonds is cashed and the nine of diamonds led to South's king, East following suit. Then comes the thirteenth diamond. What do you discard?

South is marked with the ace of clubs, so a club discard is out of the question. A discard of the seven of hearts would clearly lead to a throw-in, while a discard of the king would put all your eggs in the one basket. That leaves only spades, and a spade discard must be perfectly safe now that dummy is bereft of entries. You can win the third round of spades, put partner in with the fourth round of hearts, and score the king of clubs as the setting trick.

```
              N          ♠ J
                         ♡ 10 8 6 2
         W        E      ◇ 8 7 5
              S          ♣ J 10 8 5 4
              ♠ 7 6 5
              ♡ Q J 4
              ◇ K J 6 2
              ♣ A 9 3
```

That one may seem too easy, but when the hand was played in a Gold Cup match, West thought he could afford to discard the king of hearts.

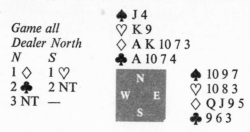

Game all
Dealer North

N	S
1 ◇	1 ♡
2 ♣	2 NT
3 NT	—

♠ J 4
♡ K 9
◇ A K 10 7 3
♣ A 10 7 4

♠ 10 9 7
♡ 10 8 3
◇ Q J 9 5
♣ 9 6 3

West leads the two of spades and you drop the ten under dummy's knave. The four of clubs is led to the knave and queen, and partner switches to the eight of diamonds. The ace wins the trick, a club is led to South's king and a club back to the ace, West following. What do you discard on the last club?

Partner's diamond switch indicates that he cannot afford to lead another spade. To give the defence a chance, put him with ace and queen. In that case South will have the ace of hearts but, on the bidding, can hardly have the queen as well. If South has five hearts and a singleton diamond he is going down, but with four hearts to the ace and knave and two diamonds he will make his contract. After discarding a spade on the club he will cash the red kings and finesse the knave of hearts. West will return a heart, but the fourth heart will throw him in to lead away from his ace of spades.

You must, therefore, assume partner's hearts to be headed by queen and knave, and keep your own hearts to prevent the throw-in. A spade is your only safe discard. Partner will also throw a spade, and will need to unblock in hearts to create an entry for you.

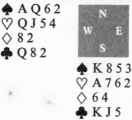

♠ A Q 6 2
♡ Q J 5 4
◇ 8 2
♣ Q 8 2

♠ K 8 5 3
♡ A 7 6 2
◇ 6 4
♣ K J 5

E-W game
Dealer East

♠ 10 5
♡ A J 10 9
◇ A K J 9
♣ A 10 7

W	N	E	S
		—	—
1 ♠	Dbl.	2 ♠	3 ♡
—	4 ♡	All pass	

♠ K 7 6
♡ 5
◇ Q 10 6 4 2
♣ Q 9 6 2

West leads the ace of spades and continues with the queen. Not wishing to be on lead, you play low, and West switches to the eight of clubs. You cover dummy's ten with your queen and the king wins the trick. Then comes a heart to the nine, the ten of hearts to South's king, and a third heart to dummy's knave, West following with the three, six and seven. You can spare a diamond on the second heart, but what do you throw on the third?

South clearly has at least nine tricks—four trumps, two diamonds and three clubs. You must assume that partner has a fourth trump which South will have to draw straight away. In that case the card you must hang on to at all costs is the king of spades. Once you let the spade go you are bound to be exposed to an end-play. There is nothing you can do about it if South has four clubs. A club and a diamond are your proper discards on the third and fourth trumps.

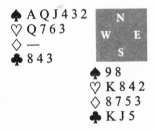

♠ A Q J 4 3 2
♡ Q 7 6 3
◇ —
♣ 8 4 3

♠ 9 8
♡ K 8 4 2
◇ 8 7 5 3
♣ K J 5

This problem arose in the 1970 World Pairs Championship at Stockholm. On the lie of the cards, East could also have defeated the contract by winning the second round of spades and giving his partner a diamond ruff.

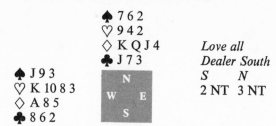

♠ 7 6 2
♡ 9 4 2
◇ K Q J 4
♣ J 7 3

♠ J 9 3
♡ K 10 8 3
◇ A 8 5
♣ 8 6 2

Love all
Dealer South

S	N
2 NT	3 NT

You lead the three of hearts against South's three no trump contract and partner obligingly produces the queen. The declarer wins with the ace, plays out the three top spades, to which your partner follows, and continues with the thirteenth spade. What do you discard?

Since he has only fourteen points in the other suits, South requires clubs at least as good as ace and queen to make up his quota of twenty points. It follows that if South has as many as three diamonds there can be no way of defeating the contract, even if his knave of hearts drops. Furthermore, if South has only two diamonds you will not defeat the contract if you make the seemingly obvious discard of a club. After leading a diamond to dummy's knave, the declarer would take his two club tricks and lead another diamond, and you would be compelled to yield the ninth trick either in diamonds or in hearts.

On this hand your only chance is to discard a diamond on the thirteenth spade and hope that partner can gain the lead on the third round of clubs.

♠ 10 5 4
♡ Q 7 5
◇ 9 7 6 2
♣ Q 10 9

♠ A K Q 8
♡ A J 6
◇ 10 3
♣ A K 5 4

```
                          ♠ J 9 8 3
                          ♡ K J 8
     N-S game             ◇ 10 5 3
     Dealer East          ♣ 7 6 3
     W    N    E    S                      ♠ 6
               1 ♡  Dbl.                   ♡ Q 10 9 5 4
     —    1 ♠  2 ◇  2 NT                   ◇ A Q 7 6 2
     —    3 NT All pass                    ♣ A 5
```

Partner's lead of the seven of hearts is covered by the eight and nine. South's ace wins the trick, and the ace, king and queen of spades follow. What are your two discards?

On this bidding partner can have no more than two or three points. However, South may not find it easy to develop the three tricks he needs in the minor suits since he cannot conveniently use his only entry to dummy. You must guard against creating an extra entry, and at the same time take care not to be thrown in to make a helpful lead.

To throw two hearts would leave you holding an unloaded gun against South's head. It is not so obvious that to throw two diamonds could be equally fatal. South's next lead might well be a diamond honour. You would have to duck to shut out dummy's ten, and a diamond continuation would throw you in. You would then have to play the ace and another club, but this could give South his ninth trick.

The safe defence is to throw one diamond and one heart.

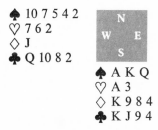

```
     ♠ 10 7 5 4 2
     ♡ 7 6 2
     ◇ J
     ♣ Q 10 8 2
                          ♠ A K Q
                          ♡ A 3
                          ◇ K 9 8 4
                          ♣ K J 9 4
```

You can then duck the king of diamonds, win the next round and exit with your fourth diamond, and South will be unable to come to his ninth trick.

```
              ♠ 7 6 5 3            N-S game
              ♡ A K 10 7 6 4       Dealer South
              ◇ A                  S      N
              ♣ K Q                1 ♡    3 ♣
  ♠ K 10 2                         3 ◇    3 ♡
  ♡ 5                              3 ♠    4 NT
  ◇ Q J 7 6 3                      5 ♡    5 NT
  ♣ J 6 3 2                        6 ◇    6 ♡
```

Your lead of the five of hearts is won by dummy's ace, and after cashing the ace of diamonds South returns a small heart to his queen, East following. What do you discard?

To give the defence a chance South's distribution will need to be 3-4-4-2. Do you see what will happen if you make the natural discard of a diamond? South will cash the king of diamonds, discarding a spade from the table, ruff a diamond, cash the top clubs and lead his fourth diamond. With nothing but the queen to play on this trick, you will be done for, if South has the queen of spades. He will simply discard another spade and you will have to give him the twelfth trick.

You must therefore discard a club at trick three.

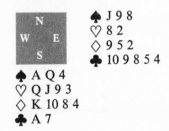

```
                        ♠ J 9 8
                        ♡ 8 2
                        ◇ 9 5 2
                        ♣ 10 9 8 5 4
              ♠ A Q 4
              ♡ Q J 9 3
              ◇ K 10 8 4
              ♣ A 7
```

South may still do the right thing when you produce the knave on the fourth round of diamonds, but he may also go wrong by ruffing, leading a spade to his ace, returning to dummy in trumps, and leading another spade. That line would succeed whenever East had the king of spades and also when you had the king singleton or doubleton.

```
                        ♠ 7 3
                        ♡ Q 9 6 2
 E-W game               ◇ 6 5 3
 Dealer West            ♣ 9 8 7 2
 W         N     E    S          N      ♠ K Q 8
 1 NT (12–14) —       Dbl.   W        E ♡ 10 7 4
 —         2♣    —    2♠          S     ◇ 9 8 4 2
 All pass                               ♣ 10 5 4
```

West begins with the ace and king of clubs. South follows with the six and queen, but when the three of clubs is led to your ten he ruffs with the two of spades. The king of diamonds is led to West's ace and the return of the knave of diamonds is won by South's queen. After cashing the ace and king of hearts, upon which West echoes with the five and three, South exits with the seven of diamonds. West wins with the ten and leads the knave of clubs. Which card do you play?

It may seem immaterial, since South has nothing but trumps left in his hand. If you are to win two further tricks to defeat the contract, however, it may matter very much. Obviously you will not play a trump, so your choice lies between the thirteenth diamond and your third heart. The right discard is the diamond, so as to ensure that when you win a trump trick South will be unable to ruff your return in dummy.

```
 ♠ 6 4
 ♡ J 8 5 3          N
 ◇ A J 10       W       E
 ♣ A K J 3          S
                ♠ A J 10 9 5 2
                ♡ A K
                ◇ K Q 7
                ♣ Q 6
```

If you carelessly discard your losing heart, South will ruff with the nine of spades and lead the knave to your queen. He will then be in a position to ruff your diamond return with his five and over-ruff in dummy with the seven, thus leading from dummy to pick up your trumps at trick twelve.

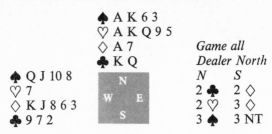

♠ A K 6 3
♡ A K Q 9 5
◇ A 7   *Game all*
♣ K Q   *Dealer North*

♠ Q J 10 8   N   S
♡ 7   2 ♣ 2 ◇
◇ K J 8 6 3   2 ♡ 3 ◇
♣ 9 7 2   3 ♠ 3 NT

On your lead of the queen of spades dummy plays the three, East the five and South the two. The spade continuation is won by dummy's ace, partner playing the seven and declarer the four. The king of clubs is led to partner's ace, and his return of the ten of diamonds is covered by the queen and king and won by dummy's ace. Next the three top hearts are cashed, South discarding two small diamonds and a small club. What are your discards?

The declarer has only seven top tricks, but it is clear that you are going to be thrown in on the fourth round of spades to make a damaging lead. It appears inevitable that you will have to give South his eighth trick, and you must be on guard against presenting him with a ninth. That could come about only if you left yourself with nothing but diamonds to lead, which would permit the declarer to score both a diamond and a club trick in his own hand.

To avoid this fate you must retain your club loser for use as an eventual exit card, which means discarding two diamonds on the hearts.

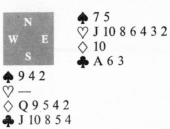

♠ 7 5
♡ J 10 8 6 4 3 2
◇ 10
♣ A 6 3

♠ 9 4 2
♡ —
◇ Q 9 5 4 2
♣ J 10 8 5 4

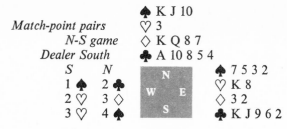

Match-point pairs
N-S game
Dealer South

♠ K J 10
♡ 3
◇ K Q 8 7
♣ A 10 8 5 4

S	N
1 ♠	2 ♣
2 ♡	3 ◇
3 ♡	4 ♠

♠ 7 5 3 2
♡ K 8
◇ 3 2
♣ K J 9 6 2

The lead of the queen of clubs is won by dummy's ace. After leading a diamond to his ace, South cashes the ace of hearts and ruffs a heart, partner following with the queen and the seven. South discards a club on the diamond king and continues with the queen. You ruff, of course, and South over-ruffs. He ruffs another heart in dummy, ruffs the eight of diamonds in hand, and ruffs yet another heart with the king of spades. How do you play to this trick?

Having discarded two clubs already you are left with the king and knave of clubs and three spades, and you know South to have three spades and a heart left. Since South made no move towards slam, partner's singleton trump seems likely to be the queen. On the coming club lead the declarer will discard his losing heart, and if you have nothing but trumps to return South will make twelve tricks by going up with his ace. You must therefore discard a trump on this trick, keeping a spare club to promote partner's queen of spades.

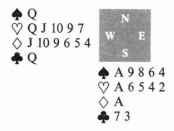

♠ Q
♡ Q J 10 9 7
◇ J 10 9 6 5 4
♣ Q

♠ A 9 8 6 4
♡ A 6 5 4 2
◇ A
♣ 7 3

This is another hand from the 1970 World Pairs in Stockholm with a minute change in the trump suit. In the event, East held the six of spades instead of the five, so that he had a sufficient defence against twelve tricks by ruffing the queen of diamonds with the six or seven of trumps.

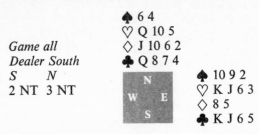

Game all
Dealer South
S   N
2 NT 3 NT

♠ 6 4
♡ Q 10 5
◇ J 10 6 2
♣ Q 8 7 4

♠ 10 9 2
♡ K J 6 3
◇ 8 5
♣ K J 6 5

West leads the seven of spades to your nine and the declarer's queen. South leads a small diamond to dummy's knave and continues diamonds, partner showing out on the third round and discarding the two, four and seven of hearts while a club is thrown from dummy. You discard the six of hearts and the six of clubs on the third and fourth diamonds. What do you throw on the fifth?

A further heart or club discard looks dangerous and a spade safe, but that is an illusion. If South has the aces of hearts and clubs partner must be able to run the spades. The danger is that a spade discard will expose you to a suicide squeeze if South's next lead is a spade. Instead you should complete your echo in clubs to tell partner where to look for the fifth trick.

♠ A K 8 7 3
♡ 8 7 4 2
◇ 9 3
♣ 10 2

♠ Q J 5
♡ A 9
◇ A K Q 7 4
♣ A 9 3

If you had discarded a spade, a spade lead from South would have brought in nine tricks whether West abandoned the suit or not. By keeping two spades you enable West to shift to clubs and establish the setting trick before running his spades.

          ♠ 9 4
          ♡ A Q J 9
          ◇ K J 6 5   *Love all*
          ♣ K 6 2   *Dealer South*
♠ Q J 10 7 5   S   N
♡ 7 6 3   1 NT (12–14)   2 ♣
◇ 10 2   2 ◇   3 NT
♣ A J 9

Your lead of the queen of spades holds the first trick and you
continue with the knave of spades to South's ace. The four of
clubs is led to the king and a club returned to South's ten and
your knave, East echoing with the eight and three. East follows
suit when you knock out the king of spades, and the declarer runs
the ten of hearts to your partner's king. East returns the suit and
the declarer cashes the rest of the hearts, discarding the five and
seven of clubs from his hand. What do you throw on the fourth
heart?

On the bidding South is marked with the ace of diamonds but
can hardly have the queen as well. Clearly you must not part with
the ace of clubs. It is not quite so obvious that you cannot afford
to discard a diamond. That would prepare the way for the
declarer to duck the second round of diamonds to your partner,
who has nothing but diamonds left in his hand at this point. To
protect your partner from the throw-in you must hang on to both
your diamonds and discard a winning spade.

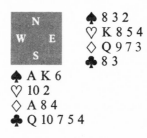

          ♠ 8 3 2
          ♡ K 8 5 4
          ◇ Q 9 7 3
          ♣ 8 3
♠ A K 6
♡ 10 2
◇ A 8 4
♣ Q 10 7 5 4

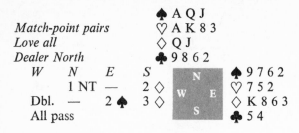

Match-point pairs
Love all
Dealer North

♠ A Q J
♡ A K 8 3
◇ Q J
♣ 9 8 6 2

♠ 9 7 6 2
♡ 7 5 2
◇ K 8 6 3
♣ 5 4

W	N	E	S
	1 NT	—	2 ◇
Dbl.	—	2 ♠	3 ◇
All pass			

West starts with the ace and king of clubs, on which South plays the three and knave. West continues with the queen of clubs. What do you discard?

It sounds like six diamonds to the ace in the South hand, in which case you are not going to defeat this contract. Ten tricks for the declarer seem certain, and all your attention must be directed towards preventing him from making an eleventh. In order to make eleven tricks the declarer would need to engineer a trump coup, ruffing out both dummy's clubs to reduce his trumps to the same length as yours.

The defence has a chance only when South has two small spades and three small hearts, for then the lack of entries to his own hand will compel him to ruff the fourth club before taking his second spade finesse. In this case you can prevent South from enjoying three spade tricks by discarding spades on the third and fourth rounds of clubs.

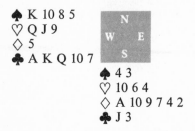

♠ K 10 8 5
♡ Q J 9
◇ 5
♣ A K Q 10 7

♠ 4 3
♡ 10 6 4
◇ A 10 9 7 4 2
♣ J 3

Note that a heart discard would allow South to bring off his trump coup and make two over-tricks.

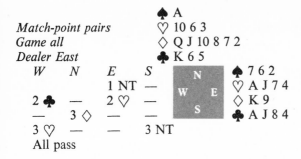

Match-point pairs
Game all
Dealer East

♠ A
♡ 10 6 3
◇ Q J 10 8 7 2
♣ K 6 5

W	N	E	S
		1 NT	—
2 ♣	—	2 ♡	—
—	3 ◇	—	—
3 ♡	—	—	3 NT
All pass			

♠ 7 6 2
♡ A J 7 4
◇ K 9
♣ A J 8 4

After an odd auction, your partner leads the king of spades to dummy's ace. South runs the queen of diamonds at trick two, captures your king with his ace on the next round, and leads a third diamond on which your partner discards the two of hearts, Plan your four discards on the diamonds.

Both the bidding and the play indicate that the king of hearts is in the South hand, so you can part with the knave, seven and four of hearts to begin with. It will certainly be advisable to hang on to both of your spades in case West needs two spade leads from you, and the remaining discard must therefore be a club. Don't be wasteful, though. The four is all you can spare. There is no need to signal with a higher card, for your partner will have no option but to lead clubs to you at the end.

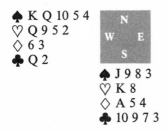

♠ K Q 10 5 4
♡ Q 9 5 2
◇ 6 3
♣ Q 2

♠ J 9 8 3
♡ K 8
◇ A 5 4
♣ 10 9 7 3

South has to discard three clubs on the diamonds, and West throws three hearts and a spade. You win the heart lead and play a spade, and after cashing his two spade tricks West switches to the queen of clubs. This is covered by dummy's king, and now the reason for not squandering the eight of clubs earlier is apparent. It is needed to ensure a two-trick defeat and a good match-point score.

South did not make the most of his chances, of course. If, after running the queen of diamonds successfully, he had led a heart from the table he could not have been prevented from scoring eight tricks.

It is a curious hand. West had more than enough strength to double three no trumps but wisely kept quiet for fear of driving the opponents into four diamonds, which can, in fact, be made.

2 • Removing an Option

There are many hands on which the declarer will wish to test several possibilities before committing himself to one particular line of play. Given freedom of manœuvre, he will arrange his sequence of plays in such a manner as to take advantage of all the available options. First he will test for a favourable break in one suit, then explore another, and fall back if necessary on a finesse in a third suit.

But no declarer can play better than the defenders permit. One of the basic skills of successful defence lies in perceiving what the declarer's options are and taking steps to remove one or more of them.

This is mainly a matter of timing. The defenders should watch out for any opportunity to give the declarer a guess at an early stage of the play. Prospects for the defence are bound to be enhanced when the declarer has to make a premature decision in a critical suit. Forced to commit himself before he has had time to discover all he would like to know about the distribution of the hand, the declarer is sure to do the wrong thing some of the time.

The most common method of denying the declarer an option is by forcing him to take or reject a finesse before he knows if his side suit is breaking. The defenders have an advantage in that they know all about the bad breaks from the moment dummy goes down. If a side suit is breaking badly and a finesse is right, offer the finesse at the earliest possible moment. Do exactly the same when the side suit is breaking evenly and the finesse is wrong, and the declarer will have a real headache.

A similar effect can sometimes be achieved by compelling the

29

declarer to find a discard at an inconvenient moment, before he knows which card can be spared.

The chance to remove an option may present itself on the opening lead.

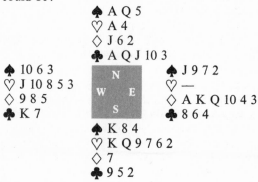

Game all   Dealer North

W	N	E	S
♠ 10 6 3			
♡ J 10 8 5 3	1 ♣	1 ◇	1 ♡
◇ 9 8 5	—	3 ♣	—	3 ♡
♣ K 7	—	4 ♡	All pass

As West, what do you lead from the above hand?

An orthodox lead of partner's suit can hardly be criticised, except perhaps on the grounds of lack of imagination. Since you have a nasty surprise for the declarer in the trump suit, and since on the bidding the ace of clubs is likely to be in dummy, a good case can be made out for attacking an option with the lead of the seven of clubs. If the declarer can afford a club loser on a normal trump break, he may well refuse the finesse and regret it later. The full hand could be:

```
                    ♠ A Q 5
                    ♡ A 4
                    ◇ J 6 2
                    ♣ A Q J 10 3
  ♠ 10 6 3                          ♠ J 9 7 2
  ♡ J 10 8 5 3        N             ♡ —
  ◇ 9 8 5          W     E          ◇ A K Q 10 4 3
  ♣ K 7               S             ♣ 8 6 4
                    ♠ K 8 4
                    ♡ K Q 9 7 6 2
                    ◇ 7
                    ♣ 9 5 2
```

As declarer, would you finesse on the lead of the seven of clubs? Not likely. Fearing the loss of the king of clubs, a diamond and two ruffs, you would put up the ace of clubs and play trumps. And that would give your partner something to talk about for the next few weeks.

A simple hold-up play can be effective in robbing the declarer of one of his options.

♠ 5
♡ Q J 10 5
◇ K 6 4 3
♣ J 8 5 3

♠ 10 9 8 6 2
♡ K 7 4
◇ 9 5
♣ Q 6 4

♠ Q J 4 3
♡ 9 6 2
◇ Q 10 2
♣ K 10 7

♠ A K 7
♡ A 8 3
◇ A J 8 7
♣ A 9 2

Game all
Dealer South

S	N
2 NT	3 ♣
3 ◇	3 NT

The ten of spades holds the first trick and a second spade is led to the knave and ace. The declarer enters dummy with the king of diamonds and runs the queen of hearts.

First, consider what happens if West wins and leads another spade. The declarer is able to avail himself of all the chances. After scoring the hearts he tries the diamond finesse and makes ten tricks when this succeeds.

Note the difference if West has the elementary technique to play low on the first round of hearts. This has the effect of denying the declarer the option of both red finesses. South can now get home only if he guesses correctly and switches to diamonds, relying on making four tricks in the suit. In practice, if West has played his low heart without hesitation, South is more likely to repeat the heart finesse. West will win the second round and continue the spade attack, and the declarer will find himself unable to make more than eight tricks.

Back to the quiz form for the next hand.

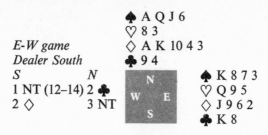

E-W game
Dealer South

S	N
1 NT (12–14)	2 ♣
2 ◇	3 NT

♠ A Q J 6
♡ 8 3
◇ A K 10 4 3
♣ 9 4

♠ K 8 7 3
♡ Q 9 5
◇ J 9 6 2
♣ K 8

West leads the four of hearts and your queen wins the trick when South follows with the six. On the next round the declarer plays the ten and your partner the knave, and West perseveres with the two of hearts on which a club is discarded from dummy. The declarer wins with the ace and attacks spades. After allowing his ten to hold, you win the second round with the king. How do you continue?

Since South has shown only four points in the major suits, he is marked with the queen of diamonds and the ace and queen of clubs. That enables you to count his nine tricks—three spades, one heart, three diamonds, and two clubs by finessing against your king.

The only play to give you a chance of defeating the contract is an immediate switch to the eight of clubs. The declarer will not be happy about risking a club finesse into the danger hand at this stage. Since he has no means of knowing about the bad break in diamonds, South may well decide to go up with the ace of clubs and bank on running the diamonds for his contract.

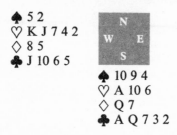

♠ 5 2
♡ K J 7 4 2
◇ 8 5
♣ J 10 6 5

♠ 10 9 4
♡ A 10 6
◇ Q 7
♣ A Q 7 3 2

```
                    ♠ 7
                    ♡ A K Q 10 5
                    ◇ K J 6 2        N-S game
                    ♣ A K 10         Dealer East
♠ A 9 8 6 2        ┌─────────┐       W    N    E    S
♡ 4                │    N    │
◇ 9 5 3            │ W     E │       1 ♠  Dbl. 4 ♠  5 ◇
♣ Q J 8 3          │    S    │       —    6 ◇  All pass
                   └─────────┘
```

On your lead of the ace of spades East plays the knave and South the three. How should you continue?

The declarer will not have fewer than five trumps, and partner's play to the first trick marks the queen of spades in the South hand. You can count five diamonds, a spade ruff, three hearts and two clubs, giving the declarer a total of at least eleven tricks. There can be no hope for the defence unless partner has an unpleasant surprise for the declarer in the form of five hearts headed by the knave. Even then, if given a chance to find out about the bad break in hearts, South will be able to recover by taking advantage of the lucky club position and scoring his twelfth trick with the ten of clubs.

To prevent that happening you must switch to a low club at the second trick. With chances of about 87 per cent available in the heart suit, the declarer is unlikely to risk his contract at this early stage on the 24 per cent chance of the double club finesse.

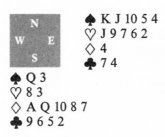

```
  ┌─────────┐       ♠ K J 10 5 4
  │    N    │       ♡ J 9 7 6 2
  │ W     E │       ◇ 4
  │    S    │       ♣ 7 4
  └─────────┘
♠ Q 3
♡ 8 3
◇ A Q 10 8 7
♣ 9 6 5 2
```

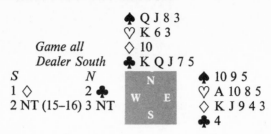

Game all
Dealer South

```
          ♠ Q J 8 3
          ♡ K 6 3
          ◇ 10
          ♣ K Q J 7 5
```

S	N
1 ◇	2 ♣
2 NT (15–16)	3 NT

```
                   ♠ 10 9 5
                   ♡ A 10 8 5
                   ◇ K J 9 4 3
                   ♣ 4
```

West leads the two of hearts, the three is played from dummy, you put in the ten and South wins with the queen. The declarer attacks spades, leading low to the knave and returning the three of spades to his king and West's ace. Partner leads the knave of hearts to the king and ace, South following with the four. How should you continue?

The declarer is marked with the ace of clubs and ace and queen of diamonds, and there can be no chance for the defence unless partner has five clubs and started with four hearts. That being so, it may seem a good idea to put South to the guess in diamonds at this point. But a count of tricks shows that this is not good enough. With three spades, one heart and four clubs, South needs only one trick from diamonds and will make his contract even if he goes up with the ace.

A heart continuation may achieve something, however. You should lead the five of hearts to West's nine and win the heart return with your eight. Dummy has to find a discard and it is natural to part with a spade rather than a club. With the spade option gone, now is the time to lead a diamond and force South to choose between the diamond finesse and the club break.

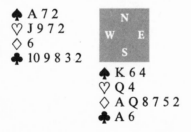

```
♠ A 7 2
♡ J 9 7 2
◇ 6
♣ 10 9 8 3 2
```

```
          ♠ K 6 4
          ♡ Q 4
          ◇ A Q 8 7 5 2
          ♣ A 6
```

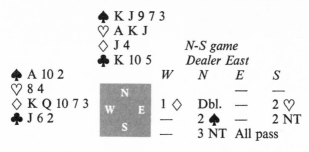

	♠ K J 9 7 3			
	♡ A K J			
	◇ J 4	*N-S game*	
	♣ K 10 5	*Dealer East*	
♠ A 10 2		W	N E S
♡ 8 4			— —
◇ K Q 10 7 3			1 ◇ Dbl. — 2 ♡
♣ J 6 2			— 2 ♠ — 2 NT
			— 3 NT All pass

On your lead of the king of diamonds East plays the five and
South the two. You continue with the queen of diamonds, East
playing the nine and South the ace. The declarer leads a low
spade to dummy's knave and East's queen, and wins the return
of the nine of clubs with the ace. On the next spade lead you play
the ace. How should you continue?

Holding the ace of diamonds and the ace and queen of clubs,
South does not need any more for his bidding. Partner is likely to
have the queen of hearts, but the position seems fairly hopeless
because you can count the declarer's nine tricks. At first glance
there appears to be little point in continuing diamonds and allowing the declarer to score a trick with his eight.

But wait a minute. South is likely to have only two spades and
he does not know that the ten of spades is coming down. If you
continue with the ten and another diamond he will have to find
two discards from the table. Denied the opportunity to test the
spade suit, he will probably go with the odds and discard two
spades, relying on the heart finesse to provide his ninth trick.

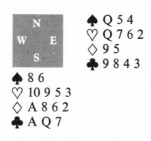

	♠ Q 5 4
	♡ Q 7 6 2
	◇ 9 5
	♣ 9 8 4 3
♠ 8 6	
♡ 10 9 5 3	
◇ A 8 6 2	
♣ A Q 7	

Love all
Dealer North
N	S
4 ♣	6 NT

♠ —
♡ A K Q 10 9 5 2
◇ 10 7
♣ J 8 6 3

♠ Q 9 8 6 2
♡ 3
◇ Q 8 5 4
♣ A 10 2

The four club bid was explained, on inquiry, as showing a solid heart suit. West leads the four of clubs and South plays the five under your ace. How should you continue?

It is inconceivable that South lacks the king of clubs, and he is also likely to have the top cards in both spades and diamonds. There appears to be little chance of defeating the slam if the heart suit can be run for seven tricks, but it is just possible that the hearts are not as solid as North thought them to be.

If the declarer is unable to score more than three heart tricks, he will have nothing to fall back upon unless he has a good diamond suit headed by the ace, king and knave. In that case he may be able to make six tricks in diamonds by finessing twice against your queen.

You should take precautions against this possibility by leading a low diamond at trick two, removing the option of the repeated diamond finesse before the declarer learns about the hypothetical heart stopper in your partner's hand.

♠ J 7 5 4
♡ J 8 6 4
◇ 3
♣ Q 9 7 4

♠ A K 10 3
♡ 7
◇ A K J 9 6 2
♣ K 5

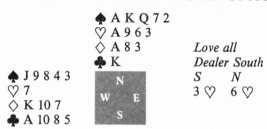

♠ A K Q 7 2
♡ A 9 6 3
◇ A 8 3
♣ K

Love all
Dealer South

♠ J 9 8 4 3
♡ 7
◇ K 10 7
♣ A 10 8 5

S	N
3 ♡	6 ♡

On your lead of the ace of clubs your partner plays the two and the declarer the seven. How should you continue?

The declarer is likely to have seven hearts, and if he has a second club the ruff in dummy will provide his twelfth trick. What are the defensive prospects? Partner can hardly be void in spades or he would have played his highest club on the first trick. The only suit that might provide the setting trick is diamonds. Partner could have the queen, but even if declarer has the queen a diamond lead can give him nothing that is not his for the taking.

On a trump switch, for instance, South will win and test the spades. When the bad break comes to light he will simply play out all his trumps and you will be caught in a spade-diamond squeeze.

If you lead the seven or the ten of diamonds at trick two, South is unlikely to run it to his queen. When he puts up dummy's ace he will still, in theory, be able to make his contract on a spade-diamond squeeze, but in practice he is sure to go for the better chance of a reasonable spade break.

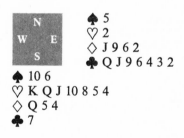

♠ 5
♡ 2
◇ J 9 6 2
♣ Q J 9 6 4 3 2

♠ 10 6
♡ K Q J 10 8 5 4
◇ Q 5 4
♣ 7

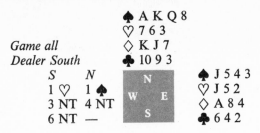

Game all
Dealer South

```
            ♠ A K Q 8
            ♡ 7 6 3
            ♢ K J 7
            ♣ 10 9 3
  S     N                   ♠ J 5 4 3
  1 ♡   1 ♠                 ♡ J 5 2
  3 NT  4 NT                ♢ A 8 4
  6 NT   —                  ♣ 6 4 2
```

West leads the seven of spades to dummy's ace, South following with the nine. The declarer leads the seven of diamonds to his queen and returns the three of diamonds to dummy's king, West following with the two and the five. How do you plan the defence?

From West's failure to echo it seems that South has four diamonds as well as four hearts. Partner cannot have much more than a queen in high cards. If his queen is in hearts it will always be worth a trick, but if it is in clubs the declarer may have enough tricks for his contract without needing to finesse.

Timing is the key. You must hold up the ace of diamonds once again, for South will not dare to test the hearts until the ace of diamonds is knocked out. After winning the ace of diamonds on the third round you should return a small spade, cutting the link between the declarer's hand and dummy. Forced to find an immediate discard on the third spade, South will have to make a premature choice between the heart break and the club finesse.

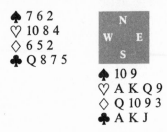

```
  ♠ 7 6 2
  ♡ 10 8 4
  ♢ 6 5 2
  ♣ Q 8 7 5
            ♠ 10 9
            ♡ A K Q 9
            ♢ Q 10 9 3
            ♣ A K J
```

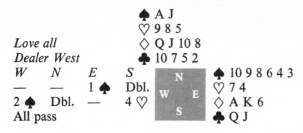

♠ A J
♡ 9 8 5
Love all ◇ Q J 10 8
Dealer West ♣ 10 7 5 2

W	N	E	S
—	—	1 ♠	Dbl.
2 ♠	Dbl.	—	4 ♡
All pass			

♠ 10 9 8 6 4 3
♡ 7 4
◇ A K 6
♣ Q J

West leads the two of spades and the declarer plays the king on dummy's knave. After three top trumps to which partner follows, South leads the three of diamonds. West plays the two and the ten is played from dummy. How do you defend?

Partner's failure to start an echo in diamonds places him with three cards in the suit, which in turn tells you that South's distribution is 1-5-3-4. Partner will need to have a club honour if the contract is to be defeated, and the king is more likely than the ace. Do you see what will happen if you switch to clubs after winning the first diamond? South will win with the ace and a second diamond lead will leave you helpless. If you win you will be able to cash no more than one club trick, and South will eventually discard two losing clubs on the fourth diamond and the ace of spades. If you duck, South will exercise his option to discard his third diamond on the ace of spades and will be happy to concede two clubs.

On winning the first diamond, you must remove this option by returning a spade, thus forcing the declarer to make a premature discard.

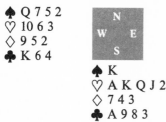

♠ Q 7 5 2
♡ 10 6 3
◇ 9 5 2
♣ K 6 4

♠ K
♡ A K Q J 2
◇ 7 4 3
♣ A 9 8 3

3 · Informative Discards

Discarding need not invariably be regarded as a troublesome chore that contains a special element of risk for the defenders. Although there are many situations in which the need to find a discard gives the defenders a chance to go wrong, there are others where it brings the opportunity to strike a telling blow against the declarer. Experienced defenders are always on the lookout for a chance to exchange vital information through their discards.

This information may relate either to the location of honour strength or to the distribution of a suit. The single discard of a high card may be enough to indicate with certainty the proper course of the defence. Alternatively, a series of discards may guide partner to the killing defence by giving him a count of the hand.

When signalling with honour cards the same principle applies as in the choice of opening leads. It is conventional to discard the highest of a sequence. The ace is discarded from A K Q, the king from K Q J, the queen from Q J 10, the knave from J 10 9, and the ten from 10 9 8. The discard of an honour card thus denies the possession of the card immediately above it and guarantees the possession of the card immediately below it. This information can be of enormous value to the other defender.

From interior sequences the card immediately below the gap is discarded. The queen is the proper discard from A Q J, the knave from A J 10, or K J 10, and the ten from A 10 9, K 10 9 or Q 10 9.

Here is a simple hand to illustrate the merits of the method.

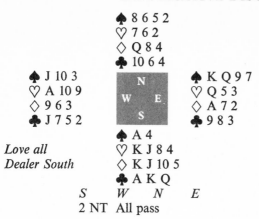

♠ 8 6 5 2
♡ 7 6 2
◇ Q 8 4
♣ 10 6 4

♠ J 10 3
♡ A 10 9
◇ 9 6 3
♣ J 7 5 2

♠ K Q 9 7
♡ Q 5 3
◇ A 7 2
♣ 9 8 3

♠ A 4
Love all
Dealer South
♡ K J 8 4
◇ K J 10 5
♣ A K Q

S	W	N	E
2 NT	All pass		

South plays in two no trumps and West leads the knave of spades. The declarer wins the second round and plays on diamonds, leading the knave and then the ten, but East preserves his ace to cover dummy's queen on the third round.

When East cashes his remaining spades the declarer discards the four and eight of hearts and West the ten of hearts. This discard denies the knave of hearts and solves all the defensive problems. East can clearly see that a heart switch will be dangerous if South has the king and knave left. He therefore exits passively in clubs, and the declarer eventually has to lead hearts himself, conceding two tricks in the suit and going one down.

If West's hearts had been headed by A J 10 he would, of course, have discarded the knave of hearts and East would have known that it was safe to lead the suit. This would prevent the declarer from getting away with murder if he held four winning clubs and had bared his king of hearts.

Opportunities for guiding the defence in this manner are by no means uncommon. For the next example let us revert to the problem form.

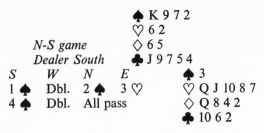

```
                         ♠ K 9 7 2
                         ♡ 6 2
        N-S game         ◇ 6 5
        Dealer South     ♣ J 9 7 5 4
   S      W     N     E        ♠ 3
   1♠    Dbl.  2♠    3♡        ♡ Q J 10 8 7
   4♠    Dbl.  All pass        ◇ Q 8 4 2
                               ♣ 10 6 2
```

West leads the knave of trumps against the doubled four spade contract. The declarer wins with the ace and continues with a spade to the king, partner following with the ten. What do you discard?

A club discard will not help partner to decide what to do when he gains the lead, and the problem with a diamond discard is that you do not know whether you wish partner to lead the suit or not. The seven of hearts might be dangerously misleading, and you should reach the conclusion that your only sensible discard is the queen of hearts. By telling your partner what you have you leave him well placed to make an intelligent decision.

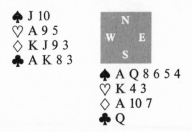

```
        ♠ J 10
        ♡ A 9 5           N
        ◇ K J 9 3     W       E
        ♣ A K 8 3         S
                      ♠ A Q 8 6 5 4
                      ♡ K 4 3
                      ◇ A 10 7
                      ♣ Q
```

The declarer's obvious move at trick three is to lead a club to the queen and king, but after your discard of the queen of hearts West has no problem. Knowing that the declarer has the king of hearts, he has no option but to lead a diamond, which ensures that the defenders collect the four tricks that are due to them.

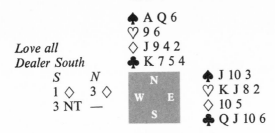

Love all
Dealer South

S	N
1 ◇	3 ◇
3 NT	—

♠ A Q 6
♡ 9 6
◇ J 9 4 2
♣ K 7 5 4

♠ J 10 3
♡ K J 8 2
◇ 10 5
♣ Q J 10 6

Your partner leads the five of hearts against South's three no trump contract. The six is played from the table and the declarer captures your king with the ace. He then plays out the ace, king and another diamond, your partner producing the queen on the third round. What do you discard on this trick?

This is fairly elementary stuff. There is no reason to suppose that partner's initial lead was anything but a normal fourth highest, in which case the Rule of Eleven tells you that the declarer has no more hearts higher than the five. West is marked with the queen, ten, seven, five and perhaps a fifth heart. It is your clear duty to tell him that the suit can be run, and you can best do so by discarding your knave of hearts on the third diamond.

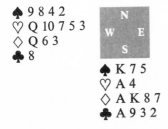

♠ 9 8 4 2
♡ Q 10 7 5 3
◇ Q 6 3
♣ 8

♠ K 7 5
♡ A 4
◇ A K 8 7
♣ A 9 3 2

Without your assistance partner might switch to one of the black suits, hoping to find your entry to enable you to return a heart through declarer's presumed knave.

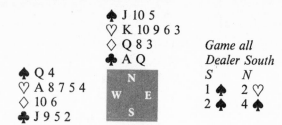

♠ J 10 5
♡ K 10 9 6 3
◇ Q 8 3
♣ A Q

Game all
Dealer South

♠ Q 4
♡ A 8 7 5 4
◇ 10 6
♣ J 9 5 2

S	N
1 ♠	2 ♡
2 ♠	4 ♠

Your lead of the ten of diamonds hits the jackpot when partner wins dummy's queen with the king and continues with the ace and knave of diamonds, South following suit with the two, four and nine. What should you discard on the third diamond?

It is plain enough that a further diamond lead from partner will defeat the contract by promoting a trick for your queen of spades. But East does not know about the queen of spades and the problem will not be so simple for him. For all East can tell, a further diamond lead might be the one way of presenting declarer with the contract by allowing him to discard a losing heart from hand while he ruffs in dummy. If South does have a losing heart, of course, any defence will defeat the contract. But South could be void in hearts and there is no need for you to take chances.

To tell partner beyond all argument that it is a diamond continuation and not a heart switch that is required you should discard the ace of hearts on the third diamond.

♠ 8 3
♡ Q J 2
◇ A K J 7 5
♣ 7 6 3

♠ A K 9 7 6 2
♡ —
◇ 9 4 2
♣ K 10 8 4

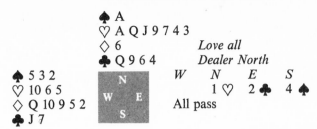

♠ A
♡ A Q J 9 7 4 3
◇ 6   *Love all*
♣ Q 9 6 4   *Dealer North*

♠ 5 3 2   W   N   E   S
♡ 10 6 5   1 ♡   2 ♣   4 ♠
◇ Q 10 9 5 2   All pass
♣ J 7

Your lead of the knave of clubs is covered by the queen and won by East's king. South follows to the next lead of the ace of clubs, but ruffs with the knave of spades when East continues with the two of clubs. What do you discard?

On the bidding the declarer is likely to have seven good spades, and at least three diamonds since East did not bid the suit. Unless East has a trump trick the defence will need to score two diamonds, but there is danger if South has a small singleton heart and three diamonds headed by the king. When South goes across to the ace of hearts and leads the diamond, East may not find the right defence after winning the ace. Instead of leading a trump to prevent a diamond ruff he may lead another club in the hope of promoting a trump trick.

You should therefore pass the word that you have no promotable trump by discarding a trump on this trick.

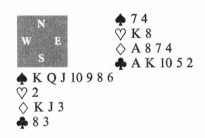

♠ 7 4
♡ K 8
◇ A 8 7 4
♣ A K 10 5 2

♠ K Q J 10 9 8 6
♡ 2
◇ K J 3
♣ 8 3

This hand is complementary to the previous one. There you had to find a way of telling your partner you had a promotable trump, here that you had not.

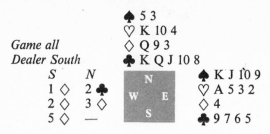

```
                    ♠ 5 3
                    ♡ K 10 4
    Game all        ◇ Q 9 3
    Dealer South    ♣ K Q J 10 8
        S    N                       ♠ K J 10 9
        1◇   2♣                      ♡ A 5 3 2
        2◇   3◇                      ◇ 4
        5◇   —                       ♣ 9 7 6 5
```

West leads the two of clubs, you cover dummy's eight with the nine, and South wins with the ace. The five of diamonds is led to dummy's queen and the three of diamonds returned. What do you discard?

Partner will need to have the ace of diamonds if this contract is to be defeated. When he wins this trick he will attempt to put you on lead to give him a club ruff. How can you tell him to lead a heart?

The highest heart you can spare would be hard to read, and the same can be said for your lowest spade. You might try giving a suit preference signal by discarding your lowest club, but even that could be misinterpreted. The only card that will broadcast the message loud and clear is the king of spades. In theory this guarantees possession of the queen, but since partner cannot have two aces on the bidding there is no danger that he will try to put you on lead in spades. The vital point is that the discard of the king of spades denies the ace, and partner will be compelled to try hearts.

```
    ♠ Q 8 7 6 2
    ♡ J 9 8 7
    ◇ A 7 2
    ♣ 2
                    ♠ A 4
                    ♡ Q 6
                    ◇ K J 10 8 6 5
                    ♣ A 4 3
```

An initial spade lead would have defeated the contract with rather less effort, of course.

♠ A K 10 9
♡ 6 5 2
◇ A   *Game all*
♣ A J 10 8 3   *Dealer North*

♠ 8 7 5 3   N   S
♡ A 9 4   1 ♣ 1 ♡
◇ J 10 6 2   1 ♠ 1 NT
♣ K 6   2 NT 3 NT

Your lead of the two of diamonds takes out dummy's ace and partner encourages with the nine. South enters hand with the queen of spades and leads the nine of clubs which you cover with the king. Dummy's ace wins, the knave of clubs holds the next trick, and partner plays the queen on the third round, South following suit. What do you discard?

South has enough tricks for his contract when he regains the lead, so you need five fast tricks for the defence. If East has the king and queen of diamonds there will be no problem, but on the bidding South is likely to have one of these cards. To give you a chance you must assume it is the queen. In any case your first duty is to tell partner you do not have the queen by discarding the knave of diamonds.

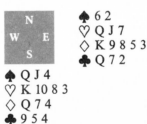

♠ 6 2
♡ Q J 7
◇ K 9 8 5 3
♣ Q 7 2

♠ Q J 4
♡ K 10 8 3
◇ Q 7 4
♣ 9 5 4

On seeing your knave of diamonds East will realize that three tricks are required from hearts. He will lead the queen, or perhaps the knave, to give the declarer a guess. If South covers, you will win with the ace, return a diamond to the king, and watch South suffer when the seven of hearts is led. There is no certainty of defeating the contract, but accurate defence gives you a fifty-fifty chance.

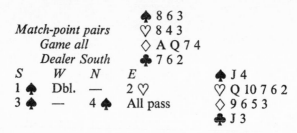

Match-point pairs
Game all
Dealer South

♠ 8 6 3
♡ 8 4 3
◇ A Q 7 4
♣ 7 6 2

S	W	N	E
1 ♠	Dbl.	—	2 ♡
3 ♠	—	4 ♠	All pass

♠ J 4
♡ Q 10 7 6 2
◇ 9 6 5 3
♣ J 3

West begins with the ace, king and nine of hearts, South ruffing the third round. South plays off the ace and king of trumps, catching the queen and knave together on the second round. After a short trance he continues with two more trumps on which West throws the eight of diamonds and the five of clubs. What are your two discards?

It is likely that partner has four cards in each minor suit, in which case he will be in pain on the lead of the last trump unless you tell him what to do. You should make it quite clear that you have no club stopper by discarding first the three and then the knave of clubs. Your nine of diamonds will always take care of the third round of that suit.

♠ Q 7
♡ A K 9
◇ K J 10 8
♣ Q 10 8 5

♠ A K 10 9 5 2
♡ J 5
◇ 2
♣ A K 9 4

South had a safe play for ten tricks by conceding a club and ruffing the fourth round in dummy. However, it being a pairs game, he properly decided to take the slight risk of banking on the diamond finesse for his tenth trick and trying for an eleventh. He might have made that eleventh trick if you had failed to give your partner the right information.

```
                        ♠ J 8 5 2
                        ♡ 9 8 2
   Game all             ◇ J 8 4
   Dealer West          ♣ 10 6 2
W            N     E     S        ♠ Q 10 9 6 4
1 NT (12–14) —    2 ♠   5 ◇       ♡ 7 5 4 3
All pass                         ◇ —
                                 ♣ 8 7 5 3
```

West leads the ace of spades and switches to the three of diamonds. South wins with dummy's eight, ruffs a spade, enters dummy with the knave of diamonds and ruffs another spade. Two more high trumps are led, partner following with the nine of diamonds then discarding the four of clubs. What have you discarded on the four rounds of trumps?

With nothing of value in either of the side suits, all you can do is give partner a distributional count by discarding entirely from the one suit. Don't make the mistake of throwing the three of hearts followed by the three of clubs. West might not then learn about your distribution in time.

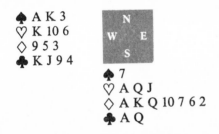

```
♠ A K 3
♡ K 10 6
◇ 9 5 3
♣ K J 9 4
                  ♠ 7
                  ♡ A Q J
                  ◇ A K Q 10 7 6 2
                  ♣ A Q
```

After running all the trumps the declarer will play the ace and queen of hearts, and if your partner has discarded a heart he will be sunk.

Note that it does not really matter which suit you discard. If you throw clubs West will know that the declarer has no more than two and can safely throw another club on the last trump. If you throw hearts, West will know that you can hardly have five unless you are holding on to something good in clubs. Again it is safe for him to throw a second club.

♠ Q J 9 8 5
♡ K 3
◇ J 6
♣ K Q J 7

Match-point pairs
Love all
Dealer North

♠ A K 10
♡ A Q 9 5 4 2
◇ Q 10 8 7
♣ —

Dbl.

	W	N	E	S
		1 ♠	—	1 NT
		All pass		

Feeling in a gambling mood, you double one no trump rather than bid hearts. On your lead of the five of hearts the three is played from the table, partner puts in the ten and the declarer wins with the knave. South then leads the two of clubs. What do you discard?

South is unlikely to have both minor suit aces and if he has you are booked for a poor score, since you could clearly have made eight or nine tricks in hearts. If East has the ace of clubs South is likely to have ace and king of diamonds and you will not make more than eight tricks in defence. A penalty of 300 will be good enough, of course.

But there is danger when South has the ace of clubs and the king of diamonds. Then he will try for six tricks by leading a diamond from dummy at trick three, and partner, not realizing that you have seven tricks ready to cash, may play low to give South a guess.

You can prevent East from going wrong by discarding your queen of diamonds on the first club lead. With the knave visible in dummy, the discard of the queen cannot be read as a call for the lead of the suit.

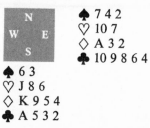

♠ 7 4 2
♡ 10 7
◇ A 3 2
♣ 10 9 8 6 4

♠ 6 3
♡ J 8 6
◇ K 9 5 4
♣ A 5 3 2

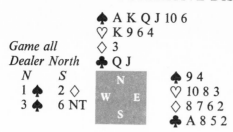

Game all
Dealer North

	♠ A K Q J 10 6
	♡ K 9 6 4
	◇ 3
	♣ Q J

N	S
1 ♠	2 ◇
3 ♠	6 NT

♠ 9 4
♡ 10 8 3
◇ 8 7 6 2
♣ A 8 5 2

West leads the ten of clubs and South drops the three on your ace. You return the eight of diamonds upon which South plays the ace and your partner the nine. The declarer leads a spade to the ace and continues the suit, all following to the first two rounds. Plan your discards on the spades.

The confident bidding marks the declarer with the ace of hearts and the king of clubs, which probably gives him eleven top tricks. Clearly partner will need to have the king of diamonds as well as a heart stopper if the defence is to have a chance. You cannot afford to throw a heart yourself, for partner might then find the pressure too great. What about the clubs? If South has four clubs the contract is bound to fall into his lap. On the run of the spades you would have to keep clubs and your partner diamonds, and neither of you could retain a heart stopper. In that case it must be right to let the clubs go immediately, for partner may also be worried about the club position.

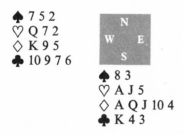

♠ 7 5 2
♡ Q 7 2
◇ K 9 5
♣ 10 9 7 6

♠ 8 3
♡ A J 5
◇ A Q J 10 4
♣ K 4 3

On the fourth spade West can spare the five of diamonds, and your last club hits the table just in time to tell him that it is hearts he must keep.

4 · Creating an Option

In Chapter Two we examined the technique of cutting down options by forcing the declarer to make a premature choice between the lines of play at his disposal. The opposite situation arises when the declarer has no choice—when the only line of play he can reasonably adopt is a winning one. It is then up to the defenders to create a losing option by offering the declarer a plausible alternative to the winning line of play.

This is basically an exercise in deception, and success will depend not only upon the selection of an appropriate false card but also upon the maintaining of an even tempo when the false card is played. The slightest hesitation will ruin the effect by informing the declarer that something fishy is going on.

One of the simplest examples of creating a losing option is seen in routine hold-up technique.

K Q 10 2

J 8 3   A 9 4

7 6 5

When the declarer leads to dummy's king, it will seldom be right for East to play the ace. If he does, South will have no option but to try the winning play of finessing the ten on the next round. If East calmly plays the four on dummy's king, on the other hand, the declarer is left with a fifty-fifty chance of going wrong on the next round.

Everyone should be familiar with what are called the mandatory false cards—the various routine situations where the defence has no chance unless a false card is played. Here are some of the common ones.

                          A Q 3
        K 5   10 9 6
                          J 8 7 4 2

When the declarer, who is known to have length in the suit,
finesses dummy's queen, East must play the nine or ten. Otherwise South will have no alternative to the winning play of the ace
on the second round. The fall of the nine or ten gives him the
option of returning to hand and leading the knave, hoping to pin
the other intermediate card in the East hand. This is quite an
attractive alternative for South, since it also protects him against
the loss of two tricks when West has the remaining cards in the
suit.

                            5
        J 10 4   A 2
                       K Q 9 8 7 6 3

South leads from dummy, putting up the king when East plays
low. In order to create a losing option West must play the knave
or ten. Otherwise South will have no choice but the winning play
of a low card from hand on the second round.

                       A Q 6 2
        4   K 10 8 3
                        J 9 7 5

South leads low to dummy's queen. To give the defence a chance
of two tricks the only card for East to play is the eight. If the
declarer can afford to lose a trick in the suit he ought to continue
with the two from the table. However, particularly at pairs, he
may return to hand and lead the knave, hoping to pin the doubleton ten in East's hand.

```
                    K 3
        J 10                        A 7 2
                  Q 9 8 6 5 4
```

Needing to restrict his losers in the suit to one trick, South leads low to dummy's king. If East wins, South will have no option but to play the queen on the second round. East should, of course, play the two and follow with the seven when the three is led for the next round. South is then virtually certain to go wrong by playing West for doubleton ace and ten.

```
                    J 9 3
        7 6 2                      Q 10
                  A K 8 5 4
```

South cashes the ace and cannot go wrong if East follows un-imaginatively with the ten. But if East drops the queen a losing option appears. South has to decide whether to play East for his actual holding by continuing with the king, or for the singleton queen by finessing dummy's nine.

When a defender is known to have a certain card, the declarer will not go wrong until he has seen it played.

```
                    K J 5
        Q 10 2                     8 6 3
                  A 9 7 4
```

South finesses dummy's knave on the first round and continues with the king. West must naturally drop the queen to have any chance of making a trick in the suit.

The problems are not quite so straightforward in the hands that follow. See if you can find a way of deflecting the declarer from the winning path.

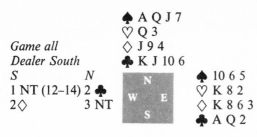

Game all
Dealer South

♠ A Q J 7
♡ Q 3
◇ J 9 4
♣ K J 10 6

S	N
1 NT (12–14)	2 ♣
2 ◇	3 NT

♠ 10 6 5
♡ K 8 2
◇ K 8 6 3
♣ A Q 2

When West leads the knave of hearts the queen is played from dummy and your king wins the trick. You continue with the eight and then the two of hearts, South taking his ace on the third round and discarding a diamond from the table. The nine of clubs is led and run. How do you defend?

South is marked with every outstanding face-card, and it is clear that the contract cannot be defeated by force. The declarer has four spade tricks and the two red aces on top, and once he realizes that he can make only two club tricks he will have no option but to take the diamond finesse for his ninth trick. If he can be persuaded that he has three club tricks, however, he will be able to count up to nine tricks without risking the diamond finesse into the danger hand. You should therefore win the trick with the ace of clubs, not the queen, and return the eight of diamonds.

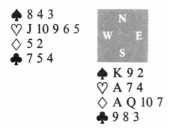

♠ 8 4 3
♡ J 10 9 6 5
◇ 5 2
♣ 7 5 4

♠ K 9 2
♡ A 7 4
◇ A Q 10 7
♣ 9 8 3

It is a virtual certainty that the declarer will go up with the ace of diamonds and repeat the club finesse, which will give you five tricks.

♠ J 9
♡ A K J 10
◇ K 6 3
♣ K 4 3 2

Love all
Dealer South

S	N
1 NT (12–14)	2 ♣
2 ◇	3 NT

♠ Q 10 8 7 4
♡ Q 7 2
◇ Q 10 5
♣ J 7

You lead the seven of spades and partner covers dummy's knave with the king. South wins at once with the ace, leads a diamond to the king, cashes the ace of hearts, and returns a diamond to his ace. Plan your defence.

The declarer is marked with the ace of clubs on the bidding. That gives him seven top tricks, and you can see that he can make two more by way of a successful heart finesse. South no doubt intends to take the heart finesse, but is trying to increase his chances by first cashing the top diamonds to see if anything interesting happens.

You must make sure that something interesting does happen by dropping your queen of diamonds under the ace. While you have no guarantee that this will do any good, it is the only chance of deflecting South from the winning play in hearts.

♠ K 6 5 2
♡ 6 5 3
◇ 8 4 2
♣ Q 10 6

♠ A 3
♡ 9 8 4
◇ A J 9 7
♣ A 9 8 5

If you drop the queen smoothly enough, South is likely to take it at its face value and abandon the hearts in favour of a finesse of the nine of diamonds.

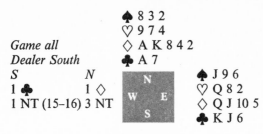

♠ 8 3 2
♡ 9 7 4
Game all ◇ A K 8 4 2
Dealer South ♣ A 7

S	N
1 ♣	1 ◇
1 NT (15–16)	3 NT

♠ J 9 6
♡ Q 8 2
◇ Q J 10 5
♣ K J 6

West leads the five of spades and your knave draws the king. South leads the six of diamonds to dummy's ace, your partner playing the three. How do you plan the defence?

If South has ace and king in both major suits, as seems likely, you will have your work cut out to defeat this contract. Presumably partner would have started an echo with a doubleton diamond, so declarer is marked with three cards in the suit. He is testing diamonds to see if the suit breaks, no doubt intending to fall back on clubs if it does not. And you can see all too plainly that your club honours are well placed for the declarer.

It costs nothing to attempt to create a losing option by dropping a diamond honour under the ace. This will give the declarer reason to hope that he can make four diamond tricks not only when the suit breaks 3–2 but also when your honour card is a singleton.

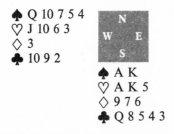

♠ Q 10 7 5 4
♡ J 10 6 3
◇ 3
♣ 10 9 2

♠ A K
♡ A K 5
◇ 9 7 6
♣ Q 8 5 4 3

If the declarer plays a low diamond from dummy on the second round, he will discover the bad news too late and will make a mental note never to trust you again.

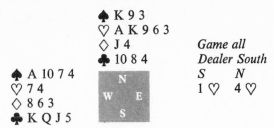

♠ K 9 3
♡ A K 9 6 3
◇ J 4
♣ 10 8 4

Game all
Dealer South

♠ A 10 7 4
♡ 7 4
◇ 8 6 3
♣ K Q J 5

S	N
1 ♡	4 ♡

On your lead of the king of clubs East plays the three and South the two. South wins the club continuation with the ace, leads a trump to dummy's ace and returns a trump to his queen, partner throwing a diamond on the second round. After cashing the ace and king of diamonds, the declarer leads the nine of clubs. You win with the knave while your partner follows suit. How should you continue?

Clearly South has the same shape as dummy, and you must open up the spades in order to avoid giving a ruff and discard. If partner has the queen of spades it will not matter what you do. The lead of either a low spade or ace and another will ensure two tricks in the suit for the defence. But if South has the queen of spades the picture is not so rosy. On the lead of a small spade South will capture the knave with his queen and will be unable to go wrong on the second round. The only card you can lead to create a losing option for the declarer is the ten of spades.

♠ J 6 5
♡ J
◇ Q 10 9 7 5 2
♣ 7 6 3

♠ Q 8 2
♡ Q 10 8 5 2
◇ A K
♣ A 9 2

South may still get it right when you lead the ten of spades, but he may also go wrong by reading it as a tricky lead from J 10 x, winning in hand with the queen and finessing dummy's nine on the second round.

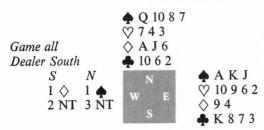

Game all
Dealer South

```
              ♠ Q 10 8 7
              ♡ 7 4 3
              ◇ A J 6
              ♣ 10 6 2
   S    N                        ♠ A K J
   1 ◇  1 ♠                      ♡ 10 9 6 2
   2 NT 3 NT                     ◇ 9 4
                                 ♣ K 8 7 3
```

Partner finds the lead of the queen of hearts and you encourage with the six. The declarer holds up, but wins the next lead of the knave of hearts with his king and leads the three of spades to dummy's seven. How do you defend?

The problem is rather similar to the first one in this chapter. For his bidding South is pretty well marked with the ace and king of hearts, king and queen of diamonds, and ace and queen of clubs. If he has five diamonds he has eight top tricks, with a chance of the ninth in either spades or clubs.

If you win the first spade with the knave, South will be forced to try the club finesse and will make his contract. You must try to make him think he has hit the right suit first time by winning with ace or king. When you knock out the last heart stopper South will then lead another spade, allowing you to score five tricks.

```
   ♠ 6 5 2
   ♡ Q J 5
   ◇ 8 7 3
   ♣ J 9 5 4
                        ♠ 9 4 3
                        ♡ A K 8
                        ◇ K Q 10 5 2
                        ♣ A Q
```

A great many of these problems revolve around the declarer's search for his ninth trick at no trumps. Here is another case.

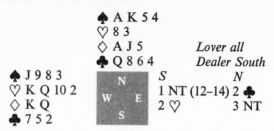

```
            ♠ A K 5 4
            ♡ 8 3
            ◇ A J 5          Lover all
            ♣ Q 8 6 4        Dealer South
♠ J 9 8 3                 S        N
♡ K Q 10 2              1 NT (12–14)  2 ♣
◇ K Q                   2 ♡           3 NT
♣ 7 5 2
```

You lead the three of spades, the four is played from dummy and your partner wins with the queen. The return of the seven of spades is covered by the ten and knave and won by dummy's ace. The eight of hearts is then led from the table, partner playing the four and the declarer the seven. How do you defend?

You have seen the only significant face-card your partner can possess, and you can count the declarer for four club tricks, two spades and the two red aces. He has chances for his ninth trick in both hearts and diamonds, and he has first tried the deep heart finesse. Clearly you should give him a green light by winning with the queen or king. This will induce him to repeat the finesse when he wins the third round of spades. Next time you will win with the ten, cash your spade and lead the king of diamonds, and eventually you will score a fifth trick in hearts or diamonds.

```
                    ♠ Q 7 2
                    ♡ 6 5 4
                    ◇ 9 8 6 4 3
                    ♣ 10 9
      ♠ 10 6
      ♡ A J 9 7
      ◇ 10 7 2
      ♣ A K J 3
```

Had you won the first heart cheaply with the ten, the declarer might well have decided to try for his ninth trick in diamonds.

```
                        ♠ 9 7 4
                        ♡ 6 5 3
Game all                ◇ A K Q J 5
Dealer South            ♣ 9 4
S    W    N    E              ♠ A K J 10 3
1 ♡  —    2 ◇  2 ♠      N     ♡ A 8 7 2
3 ♣  —    3 ♡  —      W   E   ◇ 9 4 3
4 ♡  All pass            S    ♣ 6
```

West leads the two of spades to your king, and you continue with the ace and another spade, South ruffing on the third round with the nine of hearts. The king of hearts is led and your partner plays the four. How do you defend?

On this bidding South is likely to have five hearts and he will not be missing the ace or king of clubs. The first impulse is to hold up twice in trumps, win the third round and force South with a spade. But this is nothing but wishful thinking. On seeing the bad break, South will not co-operate by leading a third trump. Instead he will cash a top club and then play on diamonds, picking up your small trump at his leisure. The only way to create a losing option for the declarer is to win the first trump and lead another spade.

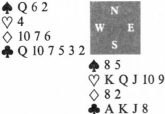

```
♠ Q 6 2
♡ 4
◇ 10 7 6              N
♣ Q 10 7 5 3 2   W       E
                     S
                ♠ 8 5
                ♡ K Q J 10 9
                ◇ 8 2
                ♣ A K J 8
```

With no reason to suspect the actual trump distribution, the declarer is likely to ruff the fourth round of spades in his hand, relying upon a 3–2 trump break.

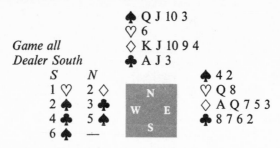

♠ Q J 10 3
♡ 6
Game all ◇ K J 10 9 4
Dealer South ♣ A J 3

S	N
1 ♡	2 ◇
2 ♠	3 ♣
4 ♣	5 ♠
6 ♠	—

♠ 4 2
♡ Q 8
◇ A Q 7 5 3
♣ 8 7 6 2

West leads the six of trumps against the six-spade contract. The declarer wins in hand with the seven and leads the eight of diamonds, upon which West plays the six and dummy the four. How do you defend?

On the bidding the declarer is marked with a 4-5-1-3 distribution and a strongish hand, but he may not be able to make twelve tricks without bringing in the diamond suit. If you win this trick tamely with the queen, South will very likely have no choice but to draw trumps and attempt to set up the diamonds by means of a ruffing finesse, against your ace.

To offer the declarer a losing option, you must win with the ace of diamonds instead of the queen. South is then likely to win your trump return in dummy and ruff two diamonds in an attempt to drop the queen from your partner's hand. The truth will be apparent when your partner shows out on the third round, but it will be too late for the declarer to do anything about it.

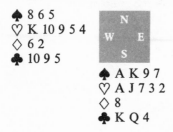

♠ 8 6 5
♡ K 10 9 5 4
◇ 6 2
♣ 10 9 5

♠ A K 9 7
♡ A J 7 3 2
◇ 8
♣ K Q 4

♠ A K Q 10
♡ K 7 4
♢ A K 7 3   *Love all*
♣ 10 6   *Dealer North*

♠ J 3
♡ 10 9 5
♢ 10 9 5 2
♣ A K 9 2

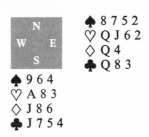

N	*S*
1 ♠	1 NT
3 NT	—

On your lead of the ace of clubs partner plays the eight and declarer the four. How should you continue?

It looks as though partner has the queen of clubs, but there cannot be more than four club tricks for the defence. Where is the setting trick to come from? If partner has the ace of hearts the contract will always be defeated, but that is a card South is more likely to have. If South has either of the red queens along with the ace of hearts he will have nine tricks. Come to think of it, even if partner has the queen of diamonds it is likely to be singleton or doubleton. You must therefore take care not to win the first four tricks, for that would leave the declarer with no alternative to the winning play of trying to drop the queen of diamonds.

The best move is to switch to a spade, giving nothing away. South may take your switch to indicate that you cannot cash four club tricks, in which case he will deem it safe to give himself the best chance in diamonds by leading a low card from the table. If partner does have all the queens he will hop up with the queen of diamonds, cash the queen of clubs and lead another club to give you two further tricks in the suit.

♠ 8 7 5 2
♡ Q J 6 2
♢ Q 4
♣ Q 8 3

♠ 9 6 4
♡ A 8 3
♢ J 8 6
♣ J 7 5 4

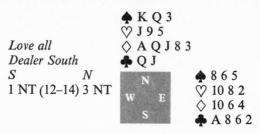

♠ K Q 3
♡ J 9 5
Love all   ◇ A Q J 8 3
Dealer South   ♣ Q J

S   N   ♠ 8 6 5
1 NT (12–14) 3 NT   ♡ 10 8 2
                       ◇ 10 6 4
                       ♣ A 8 6 2

West leads the four of hearts, the nine is played from the table, and the declarer plays the six under your ten. How do you continue?

Partner appears to have hit the jackpot with a lead from a five-card suit headed by the king and queen. In view of the strong dummy, however, West cannot have much outside hearts although he may conceivably have a king. The king of clubs will not help the defence. The clubs cannot be wide open, of course, or South would not have ducked the first trick.

Even if partner has the king of diamonds the declarer can finesse twice to score five diamond tricks, one heart and at least three spades. He is likely to do that if you return the eight of hearts, thus indicating a probable 5-3 division of the suit.

To give the defence a fighting chance you must return the two of hearts, trusting partner to co-operate by concealing his three. South is likely to have eight cards in the black suits, and if he believes the hearts to be 4-4 he will judge it safe to knock out the ace of clubs rather than risk the diamond finesse.

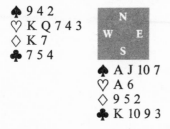

♠ 9 4 2
♡ K Q 7 4 3
◇ K 7
♣ 7 5 4

♠ A J 10 7
♡ A 6
◇ 9 5 2
♣ K 10 9 3

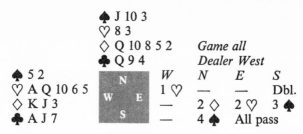

For want of anything more attractive, you try a lead of the two of spades. Partner plays the king on dummy's ten and the declarer wins with the ace. After drawing a second round of trumps with his nine, partner following suit with the six, South leads the ace of diamonds. How do you plan the defence?

From your partner's failure to keep the bidding open you can be sure that he does not have as much as a king in addition to the king of spades he has already shown. The defensive prospects are very dim, since the declarer appears to have six trumps and can clearly establish all the tricks he needs in diamonds.

If South has only two diamonds there can be no chance at all, but if he has three you may be able to offer him a losing option by chucking your king of diamonds under the ace. From the declarer's point of view, the knave of diamonds is a card that your partner could conceivably possess. South may reasonably take the view, therefore, that you have unblocked the king of diamonds from king and another in order to create a trick for the knave in your partner's hand. If South does take this view he will go up with the queen of diamonds on the second round and, rather than risk conceding the third round to East, may try to get rid of his diamond loser by means of a throw-in play in hearts.

But that, of course, will allow you to cash two hearts, the knave of diamonds and the ace of clubs to defeat the unbeatable contract.

The full hand:

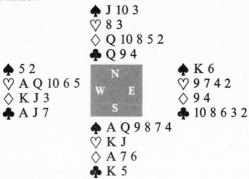

♠ J 10 3
♡ 8 3
◇ Q 10 8 5 2
♣ Q 9 4

♠ 5 2
♡ A Q 10 6 5
◇ K J 3
♣ A J 7

♠ K 6
♡ 9 7 4 2
◇ 9 4
♣ 10 8 6 3 2

♠ A Q 9 8 7 4
♡ K J
◇ A 7 6
♣ K 5

South's troubles were all of his own making, of course. Knowing you to have the king of diamonds, he should have led a low diamond from hand instead of the ace. You would then have had no scope for deception.

5 · Unblocking Discards

Another way in which the defenders can turn the need to find a discard to their own advantage is by seizing the chance to dispose of unwanted honour cards. Although high cards are normally treasured as defensive assets, there will be occasions when it is desirable to get rid of them for one reason or another. A defender who sees the threat of a throw-in play looming ahead, for instance, may find a means of escape in the discard of an honour card. Alternatively, when his partner has winners to cash but lacks an obvious entry, a defender may be able to create the required entry to his partner's hand by jettisoning a high card that blocks the suit. At other times a defender may find it necessary to get his honour cards out of the way in order to prepare the ground for a trump promotion.

The opportunity for unblocking usually presents itself at an early stage in the play, which makes the main problem one of recognition. The correct defence may be obvious enough once a player's attention is drawn to it, but it takes training and experience to recognize the possibilities of these situations in time to take effective action. At the bridge table the chance to unblock has frequently come and gone before it is even noticed.

Since unblocking discards tend to be spectacular in nature, they have received rather more than their fair share of attention from bridge writers. For that reason I do not propose to devote a great deal of space to the subject. A few examples will suffice.

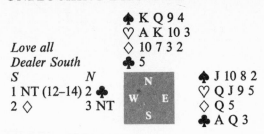

Love all
Dealer South

S	N
1 NT (12–14)	2 ♣
2 ♦	3 NT

♠ K Q 9 4
♡ A K 10 3
◇ 10 7 3 2
♣ 5

♠ J 10 8 2
♡ Q J 9 5
◇ Q 5
♣ A Q 3

West leads the four of clubs and South plays the six under your queen. You continue with the ace of clubs on which South plays the nine, West the two and dummy a diamond. On the third round South plays the ten, West the king and dummy another diamond. West persists with the seven of clubs and a heart is thrown from the table. What do you discard?

The declarer is marked with the knave of clubs, ace of spades and the two top diamonds. If he also has the knave of diamonds, or if he has five cards in the suit, he is bound to make his contract. But if he has four diamonds and lacks the knave, he will have a play for nine tricks only if he can manœuvre to lose a diamond trick to you rather than to your partner. To ensure that this does not happen you must discard your queen of diamonds on the fourth club.

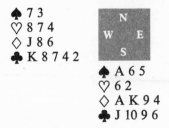

♠ 7 3
♡ 8 7 4
◇ J 8 6
♣ K 8 7 4 2

♠ A 6 5
♡ 6 2
◇ A K 9 4
♣ J 10 9 6

If you fail to get rid of the queen of diamonds, South will lead the suit twice from dummy and duck when your queen appears.

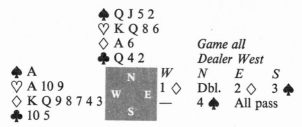

♠ Q J 5 2
♡ K Q 8 6
◇ A 6   *Game all*
♣ Q 4 2   *Dealer West*

♠ A
♡ A 10 9
◇ K Q 9 8 7 4 3
♣ 10 5

W	N	E	S
1 ◇	Dbl.	2 ◇	3 ♠
—	4 ♠	All pass	

Your lead of the king of diamonds goes to the ace, East following with the five and South with the two. The queen of spades is returned to your ace, East playing the three and South the four, and you try a switch to the ten of clubs. The queen is played from the table and partner's king wins the trick. When East continues with the seven of clubs, South plays the ace and leads the king of spades. What do you discard?

Presented with the problem on paper, most players will come up with the right answer by selecting the least likely card—the ace of hearts. At the table it is not so easy and one has to rely on logic. On the bidding and play South is marked with a 6-3-1-3 distribution. His losing club is bound to be discarded on dummy's fourth heart unless you create an entry for partner's hypothetical knave by discarding the ace.

♠ 8 3
♡ J 5 2
◇ J 10 5
♣ K J 9 8 7

♠ K 10 9 7 6 4
♡ 7 4 3
◇ 2
♣ A 6 3

South's second round of trumps was a mistake, of course. If, after the ace of clubs, he had led a heart to the queen, returned with a diamond ruff and led another heart, you would have been powerless to defeat the contract.

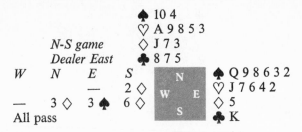

Partner's lead of the king of spades is won by the ace. After cashing the king of hearts, South plays the ace of diamonds followed by the eight of diamonds to the knave, West echoing with the four and two. What do you discard?

With only six trumps and three tricks in the major suits, South will need to make something of the clubs. If he has a club loser it is clearly desirable that partner, who has a trump left to lead, should win the trick. Your king of clubs is nothing but a liability, and you should seize the chance to discard it on the second round of trumps.

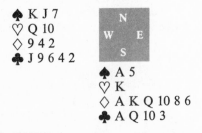

After discarding his losing spade on the ace of hearts, the declarer's next move will be to lead a club. If you have kept your king you will be allowed to hold the trick, and South will eventually ruff his remaining loser in dummy.

Once again the declarer played a round of trumps too many. If he had won the first round of trumps with dummy's knave, discarded the spade loser and led a club, the defence would have been helpless.

This is another hand from the World Pairs Olympiad at Stockholm.

♠ Q 10 5
♡ K 5
◇ J 6 3   *Game all*
♣ K J 7 4 2   *Dealer West*

♠ A 6
♡ Q 10 7 6 4
◇ A Q 4
♣ A 9 3

W	N	E	S
1 ♡	—	—	1 NT
All pass			

You lead the six of hearts and partner's knave is allowed to hold the trick. The return of the eight of hearts goes to the king and the queen of spades is led to your ace. You knock out the ace of hearts, partner following suit while dummy throws a club. South cashes the king of spades followed by the knave, on which you throw the four of diamonds. The nine of spades comes next. What do you discard?

The bidding marks the declarer with the king of diamonds and if he has the queen of clubs as well you will be unable to defeat the contract. But partner is fairly sure to have the queen since South did not attack clubs immediately. You must on no account part with a small club, for that will inevitably lead to a throw-in if partner's queen is doubleton. Having heard East pass your opening bid, South will not misguess the clubs. He will go up with the king and return a club to your ace, and you will have to concede a trick to the diamond king.

To discard a winning heart will not do. South will then attack diamonds, and the club blockage will prevent you from scoring seven tricks. The only discard to give you a chance of defeating the contract is the ace of clubs.

♠ 8 7 4 2
♡ J 8 3
◇ 10 8 7 5
♣ Q 8

♠ K J 9 3
♡ A 9 2
◇ K 9 2
♣ 10 6 5

Partner could have saved you a headache by returning a diamond at trick two.

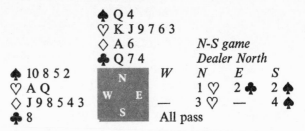

```
        ♠ Q 4
        ♡ K J 9 7 6 3
        ◇ A 6            N-S game
        ♣ Q 7 4          Dealer North
♠ 10 8 5 2      N      W      N      E      S
♡ A Q                         1 ♡    2 ♣    2 ♠
◇ J 9 8 5 4 3   W  E          —      3 ♡    —      4 ♠
♣ 8             S             All pass
```

You lead the eight of clubs against the four spade contract.
The four is played from dummy and partner's knave wins the
trick, the declarer following with the three. East continues with
the king of clubs and South plays the nine. What do you discard?

The declarer is marked with the ten of clubs by East's play of
the knave at trick one, which means you can count on three club
tricks for the defence. What further trick can you expect to make?
The ace of hearts? That is an obvious possibility, but there can be
no guarantee that the declarer has a heart in his hand.

In fact there is no need to rely upon scoring a heart trick on
this hand. You can make quite certain of defeating the contract
by discarding the queen and ace of hearts on the second and third
rounds of clubs. By getting your hearts out of the way you ensure
that a heart lead from partner at trick four will promote one of
your trumps as the setting trick.

```
           N        ♠ —
                    ♡ 10 8 5 4 2
        W     E     ◇ 10 2
           S        ♣ A K J 6 5 2
        ♠ A K J 9 7 6 3
        ♡ —
        ◇ K Q 7
        ♣ 10 9 3
```

```
                    ♠ Q 6 3
                    ♡ 10 4
     Love all        ◊ J 9 7 6 4
     Dealer South    ♣ 10 6 2
       S    N                        ♠ K 10 7 5 2
       2♣   2◊                       ♡ Q 6 5 2
       2 NT 3 NT                     ◊ Q 10 3
                                     ♣ 8
```

You anticipate a club lead, but partner surprises you by producing the nine of spades. When the three is played from the table you encourage with the seven, and South wins with the knave. Three top clubs come next, West following suit while you discard the two of hearts and the five of spades. A fourth round of clubs is won by partner's knave, dummy discarding a diamond while you part with a second heart. West continues with the eight of spades which takes out the ace and South makes a nuisance of himself by cashing his fifth club, on which West discards the two of diamonds and dummy another diamond. What do you discard?

There will be little hope for the defence if you part with another winning spade, and it cannot be right to break up your diamond stopper at this stage. That leaves only the heart suit, where you have already passed the point of no return. Partner must have some high cards in hearts if he has nothing in diamonds, but if you throw the small heart you might expose yourself to a throw-in play. You should discard the queen of hearts so as to get out of partner's way.

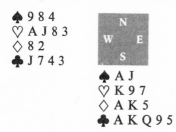

```
     ♠ 9 8 4
     ♡ A J 8 3
     ◊ 8 2
     ♣ J 7 4 3
                    ♠ A J
                    ♡ K 9 7
                    ◊ A K 5
                    ♣ A K Q 9 5
```

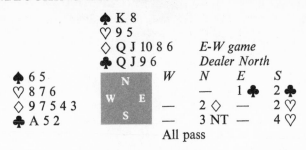

```
              ♠ K 8
              ♡ 9 5
              ♢ Q J 10 8 6      E-W game
              ♣ Q J 9 6         Dealer North
   ♠ 6 5                    W    N    E    S
   ♡ 8 7 6                  —    1♣   2♣
   ♢ 9 7 5 4 3              —    2♢   —    2♡
   ♣ A 5 2                  —    3 NT —    4♡
                     All pass
```

On your trump lead partner plays the king and the declarer wins with the ace. After a spade to dummy's king and a spade back to South's ace, a third spade is led. You discard the two of clubs, dummy ruffs with the nine of hearts and partner follows with the knave of spades. On a diamond lead from dummy partner plays the king and declarer the two. East then cashes the queen of spades, South playing the nine. What do you discard?

It looks as though you did the right thing in leading a trump, for South is marked with five spades and therefore at least six hearts. There is only one slim chance for the defence. If declarer has a small club and if partner's remaining trump is the ten or the knave, you can defeat the contract by discarding your ace of clubs. Partner's next move will be to cash the king of clubs, and a further club lead will promote the setting trick in trumps.

```
        N              ♠ Q J 3 2
     W     E           ♡ K J
        S              ♢ A K
                       ♣ K 10 8 7 3
     ♠ A 10 9 7 4
     ♡ A Q 10 4 3 2
     ♢ 2
     ♣ 4
```

In a friendly match between Britain and Holland in 1970, this fine defence was found by Jonathan Cansino (West) and Jeremy Flint (East). On the lie of the cards, the declarer could have made his contract only by the double-dummy play of drawing trumps and finessing against East's spades.

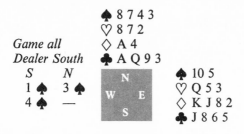

Game all
Dealer South

♠ 8 7 4 3
♡ 8 7 2
◇ A 4
♣ A Q 9 3

♠ 10 5
♡ Q 5 3
◇ K J 8 2
♣ J 8 6 5

S	N
1 ♠	3 ♠
4 ♠	—

West begins with the ace of hearts (you lead the ace from ace, king and others) and you discourage with the three. Partner finds the diamond switch, leading the five upon which the ace is played from dummy. You contribute the eight and South follows with the nine. The declarer plays out three top trumps, your partner following with the two and knave and then discarding the three of diamonds. What do you discard?

If you assume partner to have the king of hearts, South is likely to have the king of clubs which brings his tally up to nine tricks. From your partner's discard it appears that he started with five diamonds and the declarer with two. If West has the queen of diamonds you will have a good chance of defeating the contract with three heart tricks and one diamond, but if South has the queen you will need to plan your discards with great care.

You must on no account throw the two of diamonds, nor can you afford to let a heart go at this stage. The only safe discard for you to make is the knave of diamonds. If South continues with a fourth trump it will be safe for you to part with the small heart, since once dummy is denuded of trumps you can exit in diamonds. On the last round of trumps you can throw the queen of hearts, for you will still have access to your partner's hand through the two of diamonds which you have preserved for this purpose. The declarer will then be unable to throw you in and will be held to nine tricks.

The full hand:

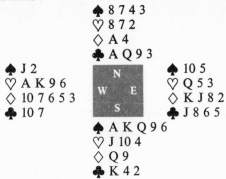

♠ 8 7 4 3
♡ 8 7 2
◇ A 4
♣ A Q 9 3

♠ J 2
♡ A K 9 6
◇ 10 7 6 5 3
♣ 10 7

♠ 10 5
♡ Q 5 3
◇ K J 8 2
♣ J 8 6 5

♠ A K Q 9 6
♡ J 10 4
◇ Q 9
♣ K 4 2

Observe that if East's discards do not follow the precise order—knave of diamonds, five of hearts, queen of hearts—the declarer can always come to ten tricks in one way or another.

When the hand made its appearance at the A.C.B.L. Spring Nationals of 1963 the defence proved too difficult for most of the competitors. What usually happened was that the defence began with three rounds of hearts, after which East was inevitably squeezed in clubs and diamonds. Even two rounds of hearts are too many; the switch has to come immediately to do any good.

6 • Exercising an Option

Methods of controlling the declarer's options were examined in earlier chapters, but the defenders have certain options of their own to worry about. The big decision that has to be faced is whether to adopt an active or a passive defence. The problem will resolve itself when the defence develops on automatic lines, but on most hands the defenders will need to make a conscious choice between the policies of chasing tricks and lying low. The success of the defence is likely to depend on how this option is exercised.

Active defence against a major suit game involves an attempt to develop four fast tricks. Conversely, in passive defence the emphasis is on preventing the declarer from developing ten tricks. The two methods are of equal merit, but only one will be correct in any given situation. How can a defender tell which course to adopt?

Primarily it is a matter of counting the declarer's potential tricks. The defenders must ask themselves whether or not the declarer, if left to his own devices, will be able to develop enough tricks for his contract. If so they must get busy, but if not they should play a passive game.

In general defenders tend to be too busy. A common mistake is to attack a suit which the declarer needs to develop himself. When the declarer cannot conceivably make his contract without tricks from a particular suit, there is no need for the defenders to attack that suit. They should leave it severely alone and wait for the tricks that are due to them. It may seem an obvious point, but this line of reasoning is often missed.

When long suits are about, an active defence is indicated. The declarer will have no shortage of tricks once he gets the long suit going, so the defenders must look for their tricks in a hurry.

Very often the defender on lead will have to make a tentative commitment towards a policy of aggression or passivity before dummy goes down. Then he must rely upon indications from the bidding as well as the cards in his own hand. When it sounds as though the contract will be a touch-and-go affair it will usually be right to make a passive lead in an effort to give nothing away.

		S	N
♠ K 6 3		1 NT	2 ♣
♡ 9 6		2 ◇	2 NT
◇ Q 10 4 2		3 NT	—
♣ Q 9 6 2			

From the bidding it appears that both declarer and dummy have fairly balanced hands with little strength to spare. West may well decide that a passive lead of the nine of hearts is less likely to cost a trick than anything else. This passive policy should not be overdone, however. Give West a fifth card in either of the minor suits and the balance swings the other way, making the long suit lead the better choice.

A different bidding sequence would call for a different approach.

S	N
1 ♣	1 ♠
2 ♣	3 ♠
3 NT	—

Both opponents have shown long suits, which makes this no occasion for a passive lead. With the above hand West should now lead the two of diamonds and hope that partner can help in the suit.

The opening lead is not always decisive, of course, and in the problems that follow the defenders have an opportunity to inspect the dummy before being called upon to exercise their option.

                      ♠ Q J 6 3
                      ♡ A J 5
      Love all   ◇ A 7 5
      Dealer South   ♣ J 7 2
    S   N   ♠ A 7 4
    1 NT (12–14) 3 NT   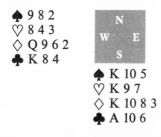   ♡ Q 10 6 2
                               ◇ J 4
                               ♣ Q 9 5 3

West leads the nine of spades, the three is played from the table, and you put in the four. South wins with the ten and at once returns the king of spades, which you take with the ace. How should you continue?

Of course partner may have the king of hearts, or king and ten of clubs, or something good in diamonds, but a lead of any of these suits will be highly dangerous if partner's holding is slightly weaker than you hope. Partner thought there was a case for passive defence when he led a spade, and you have no good reason to reverse this decision. Just return your third spade and let declarer do his own work.

    ♠ 9 8 2
    ♡ 8 4 3
    ◇ Q 9 6 2
    ♣ K 8 4
                    ♠ K 10 5
                    ♡ K 9 7
                    ◇ K 10 8 3
                    ♣ A 10 6

After the spade return the declarer may still get home if he does all the right things, but at least you will not have made it easy for him. A switch to any other suit would have presented him with the ninth trick.

♠ Q 10 9 2
♡ K J 9 4
◇ 7 5
♣ A J 3   *Love all*
Dealer South

♠ 8 7 5 3
♡ A 3
◇ Q 8 6 3
♣ Q 10 8

	S	N
	1 NT (12–14)	2 ♣
	2 ♡	3 ♡
	4 ♡	—

On your lead of the three of diamonds your partner plays the ten and the declarer the king. The five of hearts is led to dummy's king and the four of hearts returned to South's queen and your ace, East echoing with the six and the two. How do you continue?

The choice lies between a passive diamond continuation and a switch to one of the black suits. It is your feeble spade holding that provides the clue to the right defence. South is known to have the ace and nine of diamonds left and therefore not more than six cards in the black suits. Partner is likely to have a spade stopper, but once it has been knocked out dummy's spades will provide discards for at least one losing club in the declarer's hand.

Clearly this is an occasion for active defence. The contract cannot be defeated unless partner has the king of clubs, and you must switch immediately or it may be too late. The ten of clubs is the proper card to lead in order to trap the nine in the South hand.

♠ K J
♡ 8 6 2
◇ J 10 4 2
♣ K 7 5 4

♠ A 6 4
♡ Q 10 7 5
◇ A K 9
♣ 9 6 2

♠ A 4
♡ 10 9 2
◇ K 9 8 3   *N-S game*
♣ A K Q 10   *Dealer West*

♠ K Q 10 9 5
♡ A 7 3
◇ Q 6
♣ J 9 4

W	N	E	S
1 ♠	Dbl.	3 ♠	4 ♡
All pass			

Your lead of the king of spades is won by the ace, East playing the eight and South the three. When the ten of hearts is led from the table partner follows with the four and the declarer with the five. How do you plan the defence?

The club position looks ominous, but presumably South cannot be short in the suit or he would have gone after immediate discards. Is it active or passive defence that is required? Well, if South has six trumps he will score five trump tricks, four clubs and the ace of spades unless you can take four tricks first. If South has only five trumps, however, he will need a trick from diamonds and you can afford to play a passive defence.

Clearly you must hold up your ace of trumps to obtain further information. If partner shows out on the second round, you will win and switch to the queen of diamonds, hoping for East to have ace and knave. But if partner follows to a second round of trumps you will take your ace, lead the king of spades, and if that holds get off lead with a club or your third trump, leaving South to develop the diamonds himself.

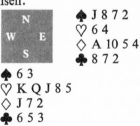

♠ J 8 7 2
♡ 6 4
◇ A 10 5 4
♣ 8 7 2

♠ 6 3
♡ K Q J 8 5
◇ J 7 2
♣ 6 5 3

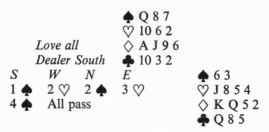

```
                    ♠ Q 8 7
                    ♡ 10 6 2
        Love all    ◇ A J 9 6
        Dealer South ♣ 10 3 2
    S    W    N    E           ♠ 6 3
    1♠   2♡   2♠   3♡          ♡ J 8 5 4
    4♠   All pass              ◇ K Q 5 2
                               ♣ Q 8 5
```

West leads the ace of hearts and continues with the king. The declarer ruffs the second round, cashes the ace of spades and leads a low spade to the queen, partner following with the four and the nine. After ruffing dummy's last heart, the declarer leads the ten of diamonds upon which partner plays the three and dummy the six. On winning with the queen, what do you return?

A heart would concede a·ruff and discard, while a diamond would give South an immediate second trick, in the suit. It is therefore tempting to conclude that the only chance is to switch to a club, playing partner for A J x, K J x, or K x x x. A club switch is both dangerous and unnecessary, however. Partner has already told you what to do, provided that you can trust his distributional echoes. His three of diamonds indicates a holding of three cards or a singleton. That means that South must have two (or four) diamonds and four (or two) clubs. In either case a passive diamond return is completely safe and leaves declarer with the task of opening up the clubs himself.

```
    ♠ 9 4          ┌─────────┐
    ♡ A K Q 9 3    │    N    │
    ◇ 7 4 3        │  W   E  │
    ♣ K 9 6        │    S    │
                   └─────────┘
                    ♠ A K J 10 5 2
                    ♡ 7
                    ◇ 10 8
                    ♣ A J 7 4
```

♠ Q 10
♡ K Q 10 4 3
◇ A K Q J 5   *N-S game*
♣ J   *Dealer North*

♠ A 9 5 2   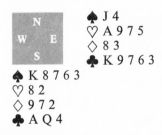   *N   S*
♡ J 6   1 ♡   1 ♠
◇ 10 6 4   3 ◇   3 NT
♣ 10 8 5 2

When you lead the two of clubs East plays the king on dummy's knave and South wins with the ace. The three of spades is then led. How do you defend?

Instinct tells you to play low in order to give partner a chance to win the trick and shoot a club back. But this can be nothing but wishful thinking. A count of the declarer's tricks will keep you straight. With seven tricks in the minor suits, South requires only two tricks from the majors to make his contract. And he must surely have the king of spades or he would not be leading the suit at all.

There is danger in the passive line. If the declarer is allowed to win an early spade trick he will immediately switch to hearts and establish his ninth trick in that suit.

You must therefore go straight up with the ace of spades and continue the club attack, leading the ten to avoid blocking the suit. As well as the ace of hearts, East will need to have the nine of clubs and the knave of spades if the contract is to be defeated.

                        ♠ J 4
                        ♡ A 9 7 5
                        ◇ 8 3
                        ♣ K 9 7 6 3
♠ K 8 7 6 3
♡ 8 2
◇ 9 7 2
♣ A Q 4

Four hearts by North would have been an easier contract, although South could have made three no trumps by leading a heart at trick two.

♠ Q 10 8
♡ 9 6 3
◇ K 7 5
♣ A J 6 2

♠ 7 2
♡ K J 8 2
◇ 10 9 6 4
♣ Q 10 8

Love all
Dealer South

S	N
1 ♠	2 ♣
2 ◇	3 ♠
4 ♠	—

Fearing discards on dummy's clubs, you start with the two of hearts. Partner wins with the ace and returns the four of hearts to South's queen and your king. What do you lead at trick three?

Partner's return of the four of hearts tells you there are no more tricks to be cashed in the suit, so a switch may be called for. But a diamond switch can hardly be helpful, and there is no point in switching to clubs since the defensive club tricks can never run away. Superficially, it may appear safe to continue with a third round of hearts, but there is a hidden danger in this course. If the declarer has five trumps a force may help him to make his contract by reversing the dummy.

Having scored your two heart tricks, you should go completely passive by switching to a trump. On this defence South will lack the entries to obtain three ruffs in his hand and will score only those tricks that cannot be denied him.

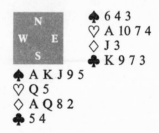

♠ 6 4 3
♡ A 10 7 4
◇ J 3
♣ K 9 7 3

♠ A K J 9 5
♡ Q 5
◇ A Q 8 2
♣ 5 4

Anything but a trump permits the contract to be made on a dummy reversal.

```
                    ♠ 9 6 3
                    ♡ A Q 10
    Game all        ◇ J 10 5 2
    Dealer South    ♣ 8 7 5
      S     N                      ♠ A K 4 2
      1 ♠   1 NT                   ♡ 7 4
      3 ♡   3 ♠                    ◇ K 9 6 4
      4 ♠   —                      ♣ 6 3 2
```

West's lead of the knave of clubs is won by the ace. The declarer leads the queen of spades on which partner plays the five. How do you plan the defence?

On this hand there can be no tricks for the defence in clubs or hearts, and it is immediately clear that a passive defence will not defeat the contract. South is marked with a singleton diamond and the only chance is to play a forcing game, aiming to score one diamond trick and three trumps. If South is compelled to ruff diamonds twice he will lose control of the trump suit and you will make one of your small trumps as the setting trick.

You have to play for partner to have the ace of diamonds, of course, but you need not rely on him for the queen as well. To guard against the possibility of the declarer holding the singleton queen of diamonds, therefore, you must lead the king of diamonds at trick three.

```
    ♠ 5
    ♡ 8 6 3 2
    ◇ A 8 7 3
    ♣ J 10 9 4
                      ♠ Q J 10 8 7
                      ♡ K J 9 5
                      ◇ Q
                      ♣ A K Q
```

East might, of course, wait to see his partner's discard on the second round of trumps, but there is little point when only one line of defence has a chance.

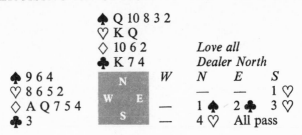

♠ Q 10 8 3 2
♡ K Q
◇ 10 6 2   *Love all*
♣ K 7 4   *Dealer North*

♠ 9 6 4
♡ 8 6 5 2
◇ A Q 7 5 4
♣ 3

W	N	E	S
	—	—	1 ♡
—	1 ♠	2 ♣	3 ♡
—	4 ♡	All pass	

You lead the singleton club to partner's ace, South following with the five. East returns the ten of clubs, South plays the knave and you ruff. What now?

Partner's lead of the ten of clubs is presumably a suit-preference signal showing something in spades. Such an indication is not a command, however, and should not be followed blindly. As usual, a count of declarer's tricks will save you from doing the wrong thing. South has at most seven trump tricks plus one club and whatever he can score in spades. It follows that if partner has a spade trick the contract is always likely to go down. There is not the slightest need for you to take the risk that leading a spade involves. The correct defence is to make the passive switch to a trump and wait for your spade and diamond tricks.

♠ K J 7 5
♡ —
◇ J 9 3
♣ A 10 9 8 6 2

♠ A
♡ A J 10 9 7 4 3
◇ K 8
♣ Q J 5

In this case there are no spade tricks for the defence but two diamond tricks instead. But note that on a spade switch the declarer might make his contract by establishing a spade trick for a diamond discard.

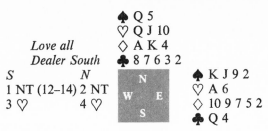

♠ Q 5
♡ Q J 10
♢ A K 4
♣ 8 7 6 3 2

Love all
Dealer South

♠ K J 9 2
♡ A 6
♢ 10 9 7 5 2
♣ Q 4

S	N
1 NT (12–14)	2 NT
3 ♡	4 ♡

After a rather unusual auction West leads the knave of diamonds. The declarer wins in dummy with the ace and leads the queen of hearts. How do you defend?

If your partner has no more diamonds, as seems quite likely, you can win this trick and give him a ruff. But would that be a sensible thing to do? West would be ruffing a loser, and the squandering of his small trump might allow South to ruff a spade loser in dummy eventually. If South has five hearts and four diamonds he must have a doubleton in both black suits, in which case he will never be able to make more than nine tricks without your assistance.

The case for a passive defence is overwhelming. Just take your ace of trumps and return a trump.

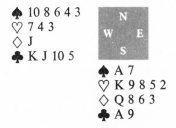

♠ 10 8 6 4 3
♡ 7 4 3
♢ J
♣ K J 10 5

♠ A 7
♡ K 9 8 5 2
♢ Q 8 6 3
♣ A 9

It will be advisable, of course, to play your queen of clubs on the first round of the suit in order to make sure that partner wins the second round. A spade lead from West will then seal the fate of the contract.

♠ K J 6 4
♡ 7 2
◇ 9 3   *Love all*
♣ Q 9 8 4 2   *Dealer South*

♠ 5 3
♡ A Q J 9 6 5
◇ Q J 8 6
♣ 3

S	W	N	E
1 ♠	2 ♡	2 ♠	3 ♡
4 ♣	All pass		

On your lead of the singleton club partner plays the ace and declarer the knave. East returns the five of clubs and you ruff South's king. How should you continue?

This is not a hand for passive defence since South will be able to discard two losers on dummy's clubs. Partner's return of the lowest outstanding club appears to ask for a diamond rather than a heart return. However, the diamonds can probably wait. What cannot wait is the cashing of the ace of hearts, for on the bidding South can hardly have more than two cards in the suit.

Cashing the ace of hearts may establish the king for the declarer. That is unfortunate but it cannot be helped. If you do not cash the ace you are likely to lose it. Your continuation is immaterial. You must simply hope that South has three losing diamonds, in which case he will be unable to get rid of them all on the clubs.

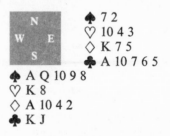

♠ 7 2
♡ 10 4 3
◇ K 7 5
♣ A 10 7 6 5

♠ A Q 10 9 8
♡ K 8
◇ A 10 4 2
♣ K J

As the cards lie, a heart return from your partner at trick two would also have served to defeat the contract.

```
                      ♠ K 9
                      ♡ Q 7 4
      Love all        ◇ K Q 9 4
      Dealer South    ♣ K J 9 2
    S            N                    ♠ 10 8 2
    1 NT (12–14) 3 NT                 ♡ A 3
                                      ◇ 8 6 5 2
                                      ♣ A 10 8 4
```

West leads the ten of hearts, the four is played from the table, and South plays the six under your ace. How should you continue?

In view of the strong dummy partner can hold no more than six high-card points. Even if he has the king of hearts, a heart return will achieve nothing since he can have no outside entry. Your diamond holding is very discouraging and this does not look like the moment for a passive return. South is not likely to have any difficulty in making nine tricks if left to his own devices.

So we are left with the question of which black suit to attack. A little reflection will indicate that a club switch can hardly be right even if partner has the queen and an outside entry. Partner would be able to return the suit only once, and the defence would score no more than four tricks. That leaves spades. Partner can hardly have five since he did not lead the suit, but if he has A J 7 6 (or A Q 7 6) you can come to three spade tricks by leading the eight on the first round. West's knave will draw the king, and when you come in with the ace of clubs the lead of the ten of spades will wrap up the suit. It is a slim chance but the only one.

```
      ♠ A J 7 6
      ♡ 10 9 8 5 2
      ◇ 10 3
      ♣ 7 5
                      ♠ Q 5 4 3
                      ♡ K J 6
                      ◇ A J 7
                      ♣ Q 6 3
```

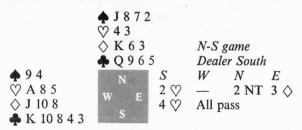

```
              ♠ J 8 7 2
              ♡ 4 3
              ◇ K 6 3        N-S game
              ♣ Q 9 6 5      Dealer South
♠ 9 4                        S     W     N     E
♡ A 8 5                      2 ♡   —     2 NT  3 ◇
◇ J 10 8                     4 ♡   All pass
♣ K 10 8 4 3
```

You lead the knave of diamonds which holds the trick when dummy plays low. South ruffs the diamond continuation and leads the king of hearts. You hold off, but take your ace on the next round while partner unhelpfully discards a middle diamond. How should you continue?

The declarer has six trump tricks, and on the bidding it seems reasonable to give him the two top spades and the ace of clubs, making his total up to nine tricks. Clearly an attack in either of the black suits would be too dangerous to contemplate. All the signs are that this is a situation for passive defence, and the most passive play you can make is to return your third trump.

Do not make the mistake of parting with your third diamond, for you may need that card to exit with at a later stage. After playing a few rounds of trumps, the declarer may well continue with the ace and another club. If you have not kept your diamond you will have to return one of the black suits, and that will probably present South with his tenth trick.

```
                     ♠ Q 6 5 3
                     ♡ 6
                     ◇ A Q 9 7 5 2
                     ♣ J 2
         ♠ A K 10
         ♡ K Q J 10 9 7 2
         ◇ 4
         ♣ A 7
```

```
                          ♠ 3 2
                          ♡ J 10 9 7 5
        N-S game          ◇ A Q 7
        Dealer South      ♣ 7 6 3
 S      W      N     E                      ♠ A J 7 5
 1◇     2♠     3◇    4♠                      ♡ A K Q 6
 5◇     —      —     Dbl.                    ◇ 6 5 4
 All pass                                   ♣ J 4
```

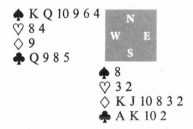

West leads the king of spades against the doubled contract of five diamonds. How do you plan the defence?

Since the weak jump overcall marks West with a six-card spade suit, it must be right to overtake with the ace rather than leave him on lead. Now you have to consider your switch. Partner may be able to provide some tricks in the club suit, but there can be no need for haste in attacking clubs. There is nothing in dummy on which the declarer might discard his clubs, provided of course, that he is unable to establish the heart suit.

Passive defence is what is needed here. You should return a trump in order to make quite sure that the hearts are put to sleep. Then you can sit back and wait for the club tricks.

```
        ♠ K Q 10 9 6 4
        ♡ 8 4
        ◇ 9
        ♣ Q 9 8 5
                                ♠ 8
                                ♡ 3 2
                                ◇ K J 10 8 3 2
                                ♣ A K 10 2
```

This hand comes from a qualifying match between the U.S.A. and Taiwan in the 1970 Bermuda Bowl at Stockholm. In one room the U.S.A. scored 420 playing in four spades, while in the other room Taiwan had the chance to take a penalty of 500 against five diamonds doubled. East was in too much of a hurry, however. After overtaking the king of spades with his ace he switched to the knave of clubs. The declarer was then able to establish the hearts for two club discards, escaping for the loss of 200.

```
                    ♠ K Q 6 5 2
                    ♡ 4
                    ◇ 8 6 3           Love all
                    ♣ A J 5 2         Dealer South
      ♠ 8 4                    S    W    N    E
      ♡ A 9 8 5               1 ♠   Dbl.  4 ♠  All
      ◇ A J 9                                 pass
      ♣ K Q 9 3
```

Your lead of the king of clubs is won by the ace, East playing the eight and South the six. At trick two the declarer leads the four of hearts from the table. East plays the six, South the seven, and you win with the eight. What do you lead now?

It seems certain that South started with a singleton club, since he would hardly neglect to draw trumps if your partner could obtain a third-round club ruff. On the face of things a passive trump switch seems to be called for, but there is something a little odd about the play to the first round of hearts. Presumably partner's six means that he has four cards in the suit, but he can hardly have a sequence such as Q J , J 10, or K Q or he would have played his highest card in an effort to gain the lead. If partner has the queen, why did the declarer not finesse the knave? It is just possible that partner has the king of hearts, but if that is the case the declarer is bound to have the ace of spades and the king of diamonds and it will not be possible to defeat the contract.

You are practically forced to the conclusion that the declarer is concealing strong hearts, in which case he must be planning to discard one or more of dummy's diamonds on them. You must, therefore, play partner for the king of diamonds and switch to the nine of diamonds at trick three.

The full hand:

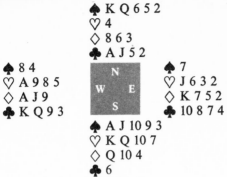

```
                    ♠ K Q 6 5 2
                    ♡ 4
                    ◇ 8 6 3
                    ♣ A J 5 2
   ♠ 8 4                              ♠ 7
   ♡ A 9 8 5           N              ♡ J 6 3 2
   ◇ A J 9        W         E         ◇ K 7 5 2
   ♣ K Q 9 3          S              ♣ 10 8 7 4
                    ♠ A J 10 9 3
                    ♡ K Q 10 7
                    ◇ Q 10 4
                    ♣ 6
```

The declarer played well in refusing to touch trumps, and his low heart was a cunning attempt to lull you into a sense of false security. If he had finessed the ten of hearts or put up the king or queen, it would have been easier for you to find the diamond switch.

7 · Discarding Under Pressure

Skilful discarding pays its biggest dividends when the declarer is applying pressure by playing out his long suit. On such occasions the defenders have to walk narrow pathways that provide little margin for error. One faulty discard will often be enough to present the declarer with an extra trick. And, since it is mostly in high-level contracts that the declarer is able to bring pressure to bear, the mistake is likely to be particularly expensive.

When you are in the grip of a genuine squeeze, of course, there will be nothing you can do but suffer, wearing a fixed smile or a sullen scowl according to your nature. It is in the pseudo-squeeze situations that correct discarding will make the difference between success and failure. Let no one think this is a small or unimportant group of hands. As a matter of fact pseudo-squeezes are rather more common than genuine squeezes. Look up the records of European, American or World Championships for any year you care to name and you will find many instances of slams made on a pseudo-squeeze against imperfect defence. There is ample evidence that the art of defending against a pseudo-squeeze is far from easy, even for international players.

The main problem is that, to the recipient, a pseudo-squeeze feels very much like a genuine squeeze. Pressure of space compels you to abandon stoppers in one or more suits, and it takes a cool head to distinguish between real and imaginary threats. To come up with the right answer you will need to keep a careful count of the declarer's tricks and make use of all the available inferences.

Here is a very simple hand to start with.

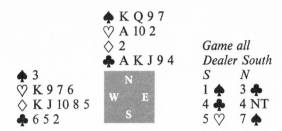

```
              ♠ K Q 9 7
              ♡ A 10 2
              ◇ 2            Game all
              ♣ A K J 9 4    Dealer South
   ♠ 3                       S      N
   ♡ K 9 7 6                 1 ♠    3 ♣
   ◇ K J 10 8 5              4 ♣    4 NT
   ♣ 6 5 2                   5 ♡    7 ♠
```

Your club lead is won by dummy's ace, and the declarer draws three rounds of trumps to which your partner follows. South switches back to clubs and runs the suit, East showing out on the second round and discarding three small diamonds and the five of hearts while South discards the three of hearts. The declarer then leads a trump to his knave, East throwing another diamond, and continues with his last trump. At this stage you are down to K 9 of hearts and K J of diamonds. What do you discard?

The ace of diamonds is South's twelfth trick, but he has no real chance of a thirteenth unless he has both queen and knave of hearts. Although partner's discards have been unhelpful, you will naturally discard a diamond. For it is obvious that if the declarer had held a losing diamond he would have ruffed it in dummy.

```
              ♠ 8 5 2
              ♡ J 8 5
              ◇ Q 9 7 6 4 3
              ♣ 7
   ♠ A J 10 6 4
   ♡ Q 4 3
   ◇ A
   ♣ Q 10 8 3
```

There will not often be such an obvious inference to guide you in your choice of discard.

♠ A 10 7 6
♡ A J 7
Love all ◇ A 6 5 2
Dealer North ♣ A 8

N	S
1 ♠	1 NT
2 NT	3 NT

♠ J 9 5 2
♡ Q 10 2
◇ 9 4
♣ Q J 6 4

On the lead of the three of hearts the knave is played from dummy and South plays the four under your queen. You continue with the ten of hearts, on which South plays the five, West the king and dummy the seven. Partner's nine of hearts takes out the ace on the next round and South follows with the six. The ace of diamonds is followed by a diamond to South's king and then the queen of diamonds, West following with the three, eight and knave. What do you discard?

This is not an easy decision to have to take. If declarer has the king and one or two other spades, a spade discard by you will enable him to set up his ninth trick in the suit. On the other hand, if South has four clubs headed by the king a club discard will be equally fatal since South still has an entry card in the ten of diamonds.

There is nothing to guide you except your partner's play to the third round of hearts. His choice of the nine can be read as a suit-preference signal indicating an entry in the higher-ranking side suit, and you should therefore discard a spade on the third diamond.

♠ K Q 4
♡ K 9 8 3
◇ J 8 3
♣ 10 7 2

♠ 8 3
♡ 6 5 4
◇ K Q 10 7
♣ K 9 5 3

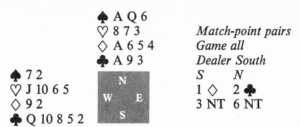

♠ A Q 6
♡ 8 7 3   *Match-point pairs*
◇ A 6 5 4   *Game all*
♣ A 9 3   *Dealer South*

♠ 7 2   S   N
♡ J 10 6 5   1 ◇   2 ♣
◇ 9 2   3 NT   6 NT
♣ Q 10 8 5 2

South wins your spade lead in dummy with the ace and runs five rounds of diamonds, on which you discard a spade and two clubs while partner unhelpfully throws three small spades. A club is thrown from dummy on the fifth diamond, and the declarer cashes the king of spades on which you throw a heart. Then comes the knave of spades. What do you discard?

There might have been some point in your keeping four hearts in case South had a singleton club and four hearts headed by A K or A Q. But you burned your boats on the previous round, and there can be no point in keeping three hearts. You are now committed to keeping your clubs in case the declarer has three cards in the suit.

♠ 10 9 8 4 3
♡ Q 9 4 2
◇ 10 3
♣ K 4

♠ K J 5
♡ A K
◇ K Q J 8 7
♣ J 7 6

When there are only two outstanding menaces it will not normally be too difficult for you to arrange to take care of one of them while partner looks after the other. The situation becomes more complicated when the declarer has threats in three suits, as in the following hand.

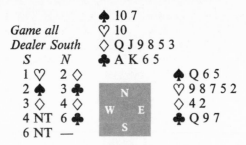

	♠ 10 7
Game all	♡ 10
Dealer South	♢ Q J 9 8 5 3
	♣ A K 6 5

S	N
1 ♡	2 ♢
2 ♠	3 ♣
3 ♢	4 ♢
4 NT	6 ♣
6 NT	—

♠ Q 6 5
♡ 9 8 7 5 2
♢ 4 2
♣ Q 9 7

West leads the two of clubs and dummy's king wins the trick. The declarer plays a diamond to his ace, cashes the king and continues with the ten of diamonds to dummy's queen, West discarding the three of hearts. Plan your discards.

You can count eight tricks in the minor suits, and to judge from partner's discard the declarer must have good hearts. West will therefore need something good in spades if his slam is to be defeated. But will West be able to hold on to his spades? The answer is yes, provided that you keep your clubs to enable him to discard in that suit.

Three spades and a heart should, therefore, be your four discards on the diamonds. There is no point in trying to hang on to your fifth heart, for if South's hearts are as good as A K Q J x he has twelve tricks on top. You will do no more than give him the overtrick, which he could have made in any case by unblocking the ten of hearts before playing diamonds.

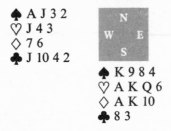

♠ A J 3 2
♡ J 4 3
♢ 7 6
♣ J 10 4 2

♠ K 9 8 4
♡ A K Q 6
♢ A K 10
♣ 8 3

I must apologize if the old-fashioned bidding misled you. This is a hand played by Ely Culbertson in the match between the

U.S.A. and Sweden in the 1937 World Championship at Budapest. In the event, East made the mistake of discarding clubs, which proved fatal. Culbertson discarded two spades and a heart on the diamonds, and the third round of hearts applied pressure to West in the following strip-squeeze ending:

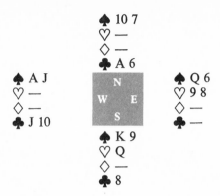

West discarded the knave of spades on the queen of hearts, whereupon Culbertson threw the small club from dummy and led the nine of spades.

A good general rule for defenders to follow when under pressure in compound squeeze situations is to keep the suit in which the menace lies on their right, abandoning the suit held on their left. The rule derives logically from the fact that play takes place in a clockwise direction around the table. All positional squeezes are dependent on this clockwise rotation for their success. You therefore give yourself the best possible chance when you keep the suit that is held on your right, for the hand on your right may have to discard the threat before it is your turn to play. Holding cards in the suit held on your left, you are not so well placed. You will then have to discard in front of the threat cards and may be unable to avoid the squeeze.

If the Swedish defender had been aware of this rule in 1937, he would have kept his clubs and defeated Culbertson's slam.

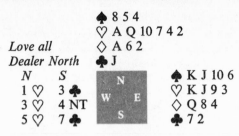

♠ 8 5 4
♡ A Q 10 7 4 2
◇ A 6 2
♣ J

Love all
Dealer North

N	S
1 ♡	3 ♣
3 ♡	4 NT
5 ♡	7 ♣

♠ K J 10 6
♡ K J 9 3
◇ Q 8 4
♣ 7 2

West leads the knave of diamonds against the grand slam. The two is played from dummy, you put in the eight, and South wins with the king. A heart to dummy's ace is followed by a small heart ruffed with the ace of clubs. A club is led to dummy's knave and another heart ruffed with the king of clubs, West discarding the seven of diamonds. South draws the remaining trumps with the queen, and continues with the ten of clubs on which West throws the three of spades. Plan your discards.

Eight club tricks, two top diamonds and the major suit aces give South twelve tricks. If he has the queen of spades as well he will automatically make thirteen. Should you try to hang on to your spades, however, the declarer will make thirteen tricks if he has *any* spade, even the two, accompanying his ace. West, compelled to keep diamonds, will be squeezed out of his second last spade on the lead of the last trump. The small diamond will be thrown from dummy, whereafter a diamond to the ace will squeeze you in spades and hearts.

Clearly you must look after the diamonds, the suit held on your right, and leave West to take care of the spades.

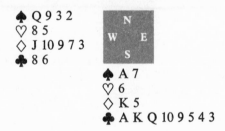

♠ Q 9 3 2
♡ 8 5
◇ J 10 9 7 3
♣ 8 6

♠ A 7
♡ 6
◇ K 5
♣ A K Q 10 9 5 4 3

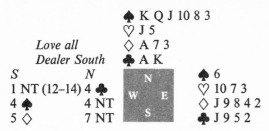

♠ K Q J 10 8 3
♡ J 5
Love all   ◇ A 7 3
Dealer South   ♣ A K

S	N		♠ 6
1 NT (12–14)	4 ♣		♡ 10 7 3
4 ♠	4 NT		◇ J 9 8 4 2
5 ◇	7 NT		♣ J 9 5 2

West leads the king of hearts against the seven no trump contract and the declarer wins with the ace. South starts on the spades, West following to four rounds while South discards two hearts. You can spare two hearts and a diamond, but what do you discard on the fifth spade?

South is marked with the king of diamonds and he is sure to have one, but not both, of the minor suit queens, giving him twelve top tricks. A faulty discard at this point could easily give him the thirteenth trick.

There is really no guess about it. If South has four clubs headed by the queen he will make his contract by a double squeeze even if partner has a diamond stopper. You must therefore play for partner to have the queen of clubs by discarding a club. If by chance your partner has the queen and only one other club, he should put you straight by discarding a club himself on this trick. When South discards a club and West does not, you can safely throw another club on the sixth spade.

♠ 9 5 4 2
♡ K Q 8 6 4
◇ 10
♣ Q 7 3

♠ A 7
♡ A 9 2
◇ K Q 6 5
♣ 10 8 6 4

Seven spades would have been a happier choice of contract as the cards lie.

♠ 7 6 3
♡ K   *Match-point pairs*
♢ A 8 2   *N-S game*
♣ A K 10 7 6 2 *Dealer West*

♠ K Q J 9 4 2
♡ 7 5 2
♢ J 5 4
♣ 9

	W	N	E	S
	3 ♠	—	—	Dbl.
	—	6 ♣	—	6 NT
	All pass			

Your lead of the king of spades is allowed to hold the trick and you continue with the queen. Partner follows suit and the declarer's ace wins. Then comes a stream of clubs, and you let go three spades to begin with. Surprisingly, partner also shows out on the second round of clubs, discarding the queen, eight and four of hearts. On the fifth round of clubs East throws the seven of diamonds. What do you discard?

To justify his bidding South will surely have the ace of hearts and the king of diamonds, which gives him eleven top tricks. If you part with a heart a double squeeze will inevitably begin to operate on the lead of the last club. East will be forced to throw another diamond, whereupon South will cash the king of hearts, cross to hand with the king of diamonds, and cash the ace of hearts to squeeze you in spades and diamonds.

From partner's discards, however, it looks as though your seven of hearts may be big enough to take care of the heart menace in the declarer's hand. At any rate this is the only hope for the defence. Your discard of a diamond will teach South not to be so greedy in the bidding.

♠ 10 8
♡ Q J 10 9 8 4
♢ Q 9 7 6
♣ 4

♠ A 5
♡ A 6 3
♢ K 10 3
♣ Q J 8 5 3

```
                        ♠ K 5 4
    Game all            ♡ K 10
    Dealer South        ◇ A K Q J 9 7
      S      N          ♣ 7 4
     1 ♣    2 ◇              N            ♠ 6 3 2
     2 NT   3 ◇                           ♡ J 7 5 4
     4 ◇    4 NT        W       E         ◇ 8 5
     5 ♠    5 NT              S           ♣ J 9 6 2
     6 ◇    7 NT
```

When West leads the six of diamonds, the declarer wins with dummy's ace and runs the suit. Plan your discards.

Placing the honour cards presents no problem on this hand. The bidding tells you that South has three aces and the king of clubs, but your partner must have all the missing queens. Otherwise South would have spread his hand and claimed. It would be easy to go wrong with your very first discard. The seemingly obvious discard of a spade would be fatal, for dummy's five of spades would then become an extra menace against West and a double squeeze would develop no matter how you subsequently discarded.

Once again you must follow the rule of keeping the suit that is held on your right. You can afford to abandon hearts because the threat lies in the declarer's hand and he will have to discard ahead of partner. The best plan is to echo first in hearts in order to give West a clue to your distribution. Then discard a third heart followed by a club. Provided that you hang on grimly to your spades, the declarer will have no genuine play for the grand slam.

```
    ♠ Q 10 8 7          N
    ♡ Q 9 6 2
    ◇ 6 4           W       E
    ♣ Q 5 3
                        S
                        ♠ A J 9
                        ♡ A 8 3
                        ◇ 10 3 2
                        ♣ A K 10 8
```

♠ A K
♡ A
◇ K Q 8 3
♣ A K 9 8 7 2

Game all
Dealer North

N	S
2 ♣	3 NT
4 ♣	4 ◇
7 NT	—

♠ J 8 7 4
♡ J 9 6 3
◇ J 10 7 6
♣ Q

Against yet another grand slam your partner leads the eight of hearts. At tricks two and three the declarer cashes the ace and king of clubs. What do you discard?

South requires just about all the outstanding face-cards for his bidding, but to give the defence a chance you must assume West to have the guarded knave of clubs. That leaves South with three spades, three hearts, three diamonds and two clubs making a total of eleven tricks. Unhappily, you must unguard one of your suits immediately, which is likely to give South a twelfth trick.

The rule about keeping the suit held on your right does not apply here, for it is clear that partner cannot guard any suit except clubs. In fact the only safe discard you can make is a diamond. Anything else runs the risk of enabling the declarer to squeeze you again by the play of the winner established by your discard. The diamond discard is safe because the declarer has no communications in the other suits. By the time the fourth diamond is played all squeeze positions will have been lost.

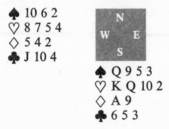

♠ 10 6 2
♡ 8 7 5 4
◇ 5 4 2
♣ J 10 4

♠ Q 9 5 3
♡ K Q 10 2
◇ A 9
♣ 6 5 3

♠ Q 10 8 6
♡ J 4 3
◇ 3 2   Love all
♣ K 5 4 3   Dealer South

♠ 9 7 4 3   S   N
♡ 9 6 5   2 NT 3 ♣
◇ A 9 8 5 4   3 ♡ 3 NT
♣ 2

On your lead of the five of diamonds partner plays the king and declarer the ten. East returns the seven of diamonds to South's queen and your four. Next comes the ace of clubs, East playing the knave, followed by the queen of clubs. What do you discard?

It is clear that you can safely discard a spade, since your holding in this suit is not likely to make any contribution to the defence. It may not be so clear that a spade is the only card you can afford to discard. The declarer's next move could well be to exit with the knave of diamonds. Since any switch would be fraught with danger you would have to run the suit, and this could embarrass your partner if he has stoppers in each of the other suits. If you had discarded his task might be impossible.

♠ K J 2
♡ Q 10 7
◇ K 7 6
♣ J 10 9 8

♠ A 5
♡ A K 8 2
◇ Q J 10
♣ A Q 7 6

On the diamonds South would discard two spades and a heart from dummy and a club and a spade from hand. If East throws a heart on the last diamond he concedes two tricks at a stroke. If he discards a second spade, or a club, he will suffer again when the established winner is cashed. By keeping your hearts, however, you nullify the threat of the heart suit and ensure the defeat of the game.

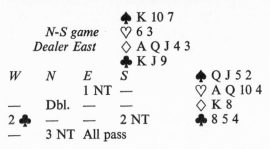

On partner's lead of the three of clubs the declarer plays the knave from dummy and the ten from his own hand. At trick two the three of hearts is led from the table. Since it would clearly be dangerous to allow South to make an early heart trick and switch to diamonds, you go up with the ace and return partner's suit. On the eight of clubs South plays the queen and West the two. After a moment's thought, the declarer overtakes with dummy's king and continues with the nine of clubs on which he throws a diamond. Partner takes his ace and leads another club, on which you throw a spade while diamonds are discarded from dummy and the declarer's hand. Yet another diamond is discarded from dummy on the last club. What do you discard?

The declarer knows that you have the outstanding honour cards and he will certainly not attempt the diamond finesse. He is likely to have the ace of spades and the king and knave of hearts, which gives him no more than seven tricks with the aid of the heart finesse. You are in the grip of a triple squeeze, however, if the declarer has four hearts, which seems probable from his early play. The problem is to prevent the squeeze from repeating and thus gaining two tricks for the declarer.

There is no hope if the declarer has the nine of spades, but if your partner has that card the combination of a good discard from you and an intelligent switch by West might just do the trick. You must discard another spade and hope that West will find the lead of a heart to break communications between the declarer and dummy.

The full hand:

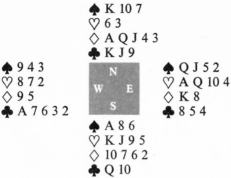

♠ K 10 7
♡ 6 3
◇ A Q J 4 3
♣ K J 9

♠ 9 4 3
♡ 8 7 2
◇ 9 5
♣ A 7 6 3 2

♠ Q J 5 2
♡ A Q 10 4
◇ K 8
♣ 8 5 4

♠ A 8 6
♡ K J 9 5
◇ 10 7 6 2
♣ Q 10

After the heart switch South has no further play for his contract. He wins the king and knave of hearts, but is unable to cash the winner established by your discard without cutting the last link between his hand and dummy.

Any other discard by East permits the contract to be made.

8 • Preserving an Option

Defenders who have learned to appreciate the deadly effect of an attack on the declarer's options will be quick to realize the value of preserving their own.

In the course of the early play when an accurate count of the hand is not yet available, there will often be some doubt about the best method of pressing home the attack. Usually there will be more than one possible high-card holding for the declarer or more than one possible distribution to take into account. What constitutes an adequate defence against one such holding may be catastrophic against another. For this reason the experienced defender tries to avoid making any irrevocable commitment at an early stage. He prefers to hedge his bet by looking for a play that keeps all the defensive options open.

Often this is merely a matter of trying everything in the proper order. Faced with a choice between two tempting lines of defence, a player should first try the one which will not inevitably present the declarer with his contract if it fails. There may, of course, be no way of retaining all the options. Sooner or later in every hand there comes a point where the defenders have to commit themselves. But in order to keep guesswork to a minimum the aim should be to delay this moment for as long as possible.

Before making any play, however obvious it may seem, the defenders should look closely at the position and ask themselves if there is any possibility they have overlooked. If so, they must search for a means of catering for this chance as well as the more likely ones. Defensive safety plays are not so very rare.

Here is a simple example of the kind of reasoning that is required.

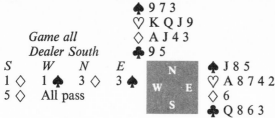

```
                    ♠ 9 7 3
                    ♡ K Q J 9
    Game all        ◊ A J 4 3
    Dealer South    ♣ 9 5
S     W     N     E           ♠ J 8 5
1 ◊   1 ♠   3 ◊   3 ♠         ♡ A 8 7 4 2
5 ◊   All pass                ◊ 6
                              ♣ Q 8 6 3
```

The opening lead of the king of spades is won by South with the ace. After cashing the king of diamonds, on which partner plays the seven, the declarer leads the five of hearts. West plays the three and dummy the king, and you win with the ace. How should you continue?

It looks as though the declarer has seven diamonds which, with three hearts and the ace of spades, will give him eleven tricks as soon as he regains the lead unless you can cash some fast tricks. There may or may not be a trick to cash in spades, but there cannot be two, since partner would not make a vulnerable overcall in a four card suit. You are therefore forced to rely on partner for the ace of clubs, in which case it must be right to return the three of clubs rather than a spade.

The club return keeps your options open, ensuring the defeat of the contract when partner has the ace of clubs and a spade trick and also when he has ace and knave of clubs. With the king of clubs instead of the queen, you would, of course, lead the king to put partner in the picture.

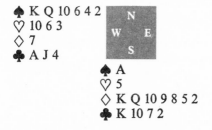

```
♠ K Q 10 6 4 2
♡ 10 6 3
◊ 7
♣ A J 4
            ♠ A
            ♡ 5
            ◊ K Q 10 9 8 5 2
            ♣ K 10 7 2
```

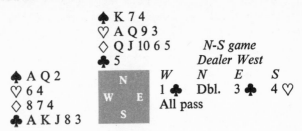

♠ K 7 4
♡ A Q 9 3
◇ Q J 10 6 5   *N-S game*
♣ 5   *Dealer West*

♠ A Q 2
♡ 6 4
◇ 8 7 4
♣ A K J 8 3

W	N	E	S
1♣	Dbl.	3♣	4♡
All pass			

On your lead of the ace of clubs your partner plays the two and the declarer the four. How should you continue?

There is clearly no hope of defeating this contract unless your partner has a trick in one of the red suits, either the king of hearts or the ace of diamonds. East can hardly have both of these cards in view of the declarer's strong bidding. The other two defensive tricks will therefore need to come from spades, and the suit must be attacked before partner's red stopper is forced out.

An immediate switch to the two of spades, or a lead of the ace followed by the two, will be good enough if your partner has the knave of spades, but is there any need to commit yourself to that particular holding? A little reflection will tell you that partner does not need the knave of spades to defeat the contract. A holding of the ten and nine will serve just as well.

The safe defence that caters for partner holding either the knave or the ten and nine of spades is a switch to the queen of spades at trick two.

♠ 10 9 6 3
♡ K 7
◇ 9 2
♣ Q 10 9 6 2

♠ J 8 5
♡ J 10 8 5 2
◇ A K 3
♣ 7 4

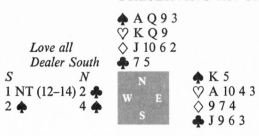

Love all
Dealer South

♠ A Q 9 3
♡ K Q 9
◇ J 10 6 2
♣ 7 5

♠ K 5
♡ A 10 4 3
◇ 9 7 4
♣ J 9 6 3

S	N
1 NT (12–14)	2 ♣
2 ♠	4 ♠

West leads the two of clubs and your knave is captured by the ace. The declarer leads the knave of spades on which partner plays the seven, dummy the three and you the king. How should you continue?

Since the declarer is marked with the king of clubs it is clear that you need three tricks in the red suits to beat the contract. The best chance is that partner has two diamond tricks, but there is also a possibility of scoring two heart tricks if West has the knave. The trouble with a diamond lead at this point is that it commits you irrevocably to playing for partner to have two tricks in the suit. If it turns out that he has only one, it will be too late to switch the attack to hearts. The play to the first two tricks marks the declarer with no more than six cards in the red suits, and he will be able to discard his second heart loser on the diamonds once partner's stopper has gone.

To keep the options open you must first try the lead of the three of hearts. If partner does not have the knave no damage will be done, for you can still win the second round of hearts and try for two diamond tricks.

♠ 7 6 2
♡ J 6 5
◇ A 8 3
♣ Q 10 8 2

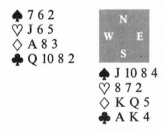

♠ J 10 8 4
♡ 8 7 2
◇ K Q 5
♣ A K 4

♠ J 7
♡ A K Q J 4
◇ A Q 6 3   *Love all*
♣ Q 8   *Dealer North*

♠ A 8 4 2   N   S
♡ 10 6 3   1 ♡   1 ♠
◇ 9 8   3 ◇   3 NT
♣ K J 6 4

You lead the four of clubs against South's three no trump contract. When the queen is played from the table you fear the worst, but partner produces the ace and the declarer follows with the two. East returns the seven of clubs, South plays the three, and you win the trick with the knave. How should you continue?

Since the declarer appears to have a stopper in the nine and ten of clubs you will have to look elsewhere for the setting trick. It seems natural to switch to a diamond in the hope of finding partner with the king, but sober reflection should convince you that this is unwise. If the declarer has the king of diamonds, a diamond switch may enable him to run nine straight tricks.

To avail yourself of all the options you should lead a small spade. This cannot cost the contract even if partner has nothing in spades. In that case you will win the second round of spades and switch to diamonds, and the declarer will still be unable to make nine tricks if your partner has the king.

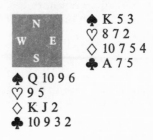

♠ K 5 3
♡ 8 7 2
◇ 10 7 5 4
♣ A 7 5

♠ Q 10 9 6
♡ 9 5
◇ K J 2
♣ 10 9 3 2

♠ Q J 9 3
♡ 4
◇ A K 10 9 6   *Game all*
♣ K 8 3   *Dealer West*

♠ A 6
♡ A K Q 7 5
◇ Q J 7 5 2
♣ A

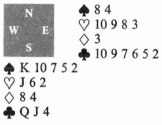

W	N	E	S
1 ♡	Dbl.	2 ♡	2 ♠
4 ♡	4 ♠	—	—
Dbl.	All pass		

On your lead of the ace of clubs partner plays the two and declarer the four. How should you continue?

The defence that first suggests itself is to put East on lead with the knave of hearts to give you a club ruff. No great significance can be attached to partner's two of clubs, for he would not consider the knave of hearts to be an entry. Nevertheless, if East does not have the knave of hearts an underlead will permit the declarer to make an overtrick.

There is no need to commit yourself so soon. Since you have trump control it must be safe to lead a diamond first. South can hardly have a diamond void and a doubleton heart or he would have bid more strongly. If East follows to the diamond lead with a card that could be the start of an echo, you will still have a critical decision to make when in with the ace of spades. But if he plays the lowest outstanding diamond you will know it for a singleton, and the way will be clear to a score of plus 500 instead of minus 990.

♠ 8 4
♡ 10 9 8 3
◇ 3
♣ 10 9 7 6 5 2

♠ K 10 7 5 2
♡ J 6 2
◇ 8 4
♣ Q J 4

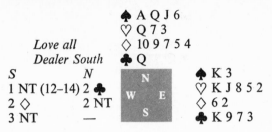

```
                          ♠ A Q J 6
                          ♡ Q 7 3
        Love all          ◇ 10 9 7 5 4
        Dealer South      ♣ Q
   S              N            N          ♠ K 3
   1 NT (12–14)  2 ♣                      ♡ K J 8 5 2
                          W       E
   2 ◇           2 NT                     ◇ 6 2
                              S
   3 NT           —                       ♣ K 9 7 3
```

Partner gives you a pleasant surprise when he leads the ten of hearts against South's three no trump contract. The three is played from the table, you encourage with the eight, and the declarer wins with the ace. The ten of spades is led and run to your king. What do you lead now?

You have only to find your partner's entry to enjoy four further tricks in hearts. It is natural to place West with something in diamonds, but to lead a diamond at this point would be to put all the defensive eggs in the one basket. There is no need to bank on your partner having a diamond stopper. The contract can be defeated with absolute certainty if only you test the various possibilities in the proper order.

Your first move should be a lead of the seven of clubs. If South has the ace this will allow him to make two club tricks. But since partner will then be marked with the ace or king of diamonds, the declarer will be unable to make more than seven tricks altogether. And if partner has the ace of clubs, of course, the contract will go three down on his heart return.

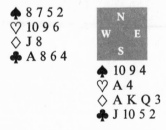

```
   ♠ 8 7 5 2
   ♡ 10 9 6            N
   ◇ J 8          W         E
   ♣ A 8 6 4           S
                   ♠ 10 9 4
                   ♡ A 4
                   ◇ A K Q 3
                   ♣ J 10 5 2
```

♠ Q 6
♡ A K Q J
◇ 9 6 5   *Game all*
♣ K J 9 3   *Dealer North*

♠ A 5 2   N   S
♡ 3 2   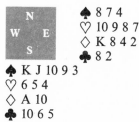   1 ♡   1 ♠
◇ Q J 7 3   2 ♣   2 ♠
♣ A Q 7 4   3 ♠   4 ♠

On your lead of the queen of diamonds your partner plays the eight and the declarer the ace. A spade is led to the queen and a spade returned to South's knave, East echoing with the eight and four. After taking your ace how should you continue?

It looks as if your partner has the king of diamonds, in which case you may be able to cash two diamond tricks and the ace of clubs to defeat the contract. But suppose there is only one diamond trick for the defence. Is there anything else worth trying? Well, the trump echo tells you that partner has three trumps. If he also has four diamonds and four hearts he will have a doubleton club, and you will be able to engineer a club ruff provided that you can prevent the declarer reaching his hand to draw trumps.

It would therefore be a mistake to lead a second round of diamonds at this point. First you must try the clubs, leading the queen to lock the declarer in dummy. If partner echoes in clubs you will give him his ruff. Otherwise you can try to cash two diamonds.

♠ 8 7 4
♡ 10 9 8 7
◇ K 8 4 2
♣ 8 2

♠ K J 10 9 3
♡ 6 5 4
◇ A 10
♣ 10 6 5

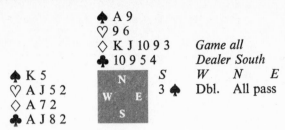

♠ A 9
♡ 9 6
◇ K J 10 9 3   *Game all*
♣ 10 9 5 4   *Dealer South*

♠ K 5
♡ A J 5 2
◇ A 7 2
♣ A J 8 2

S	W	N	E
3 ♠	Dbl.	All pass	

You lead the ace of hearts and wince at the sight of the trump ace in dummy. However, East plays the eight of hearts and you continue with a second round to his king, South following with the ten and the queen. East switches to the six of clubs and South plays the king. How do you defend?

The club lead may be from three to the queen, in which case you can win the ace and return the two, eventually scoring the setting trick with the diamond ace. Alternatively, the six of clubs may be a singleton. In that case declarer will be void in diamonds and you will need two club tricks and a club ruff to beat him. Again it is a sufficient defence to win the ace of clubs and return another club.

But if partner has led from a doubleton it will not be good enough to return the two of clubs. The declarer will win in hand with the seven, draw trumps finessing against your king, and claim his contract. To keep all the options open you must return the eight of clubs instead of the two. With the lead placed in dummy, South will be unable to draw trumps immediately and will have to lead a diamond, whereupon you will win with the ace and give your partner a club ruff.

♠ 4 3
♡ K 8 7 4 3
◇ Q 8 5 4
♣ 6 3

♠ Q J 10 8 7 6 2
♡ Q 10
◇ 6
♣ K Q 7

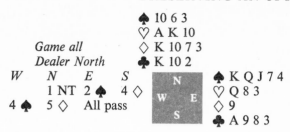

```
                    ♠ 10 6 3
                    ♡ A K 10
        Game all     ◇ K 10 7 3
        Dealer North ♣ K 10 2
  W    N    E    S              ♠ K Q J 7 4
       1 NT 2 ♠  4 ◇            ♡ Q 8 3
  4 ♠  5 ◇  All pass           ◇ 9
                               ♣ A 9 8 3
```

West leads the ace of spades, on which you play the four and the declarer the nine. As you had hoped, West switches to the queen of clubs. The king is played from dummy and South plays the five under your ace. How should you continue?

It is plain that the contract cannot be made, for even if the declarer has eight trumps, he must have a loser left in one of the side suits. Nevertheless, it is easy to lose an option through carelessness. An attempt to give partner a second club trick will lead to disaster if South has no more clubs but has concealed the eight of spades. Eight rounds of trumps would generate an eleventh trick by means of a double squeeze. West would have to hang on to his knave of clubs and you would have to keep a spade, and neither of you would be able to retain a heart guard.

A switch back to spades, on the other hand, is completely safe even if declarer has a losing club and no more spades. With the spade position clarified, you can keep hearts and spades behind dummy and your partner can happily throw his hearts so that no squeeze will be possible.

```
        ♠ A 5 2
        ♡ J 7 6 4 2
        ◇ —
        ♣ Q J 7 6 4
                       ♠ 9 8
                       ♡ 9 5
                       ◇ A Q J 8 6 5 4 2
                       ♣ 5
```

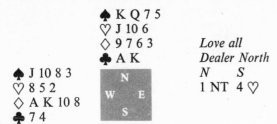

♠ K Q 7 5
♡ J 10 6
◇ 9 7 6 3
♣ A K

Love all
Dealer North

N   S
1 NT   4 ♡

♠ J 10 8 3
♡ 8 5 2
◇ A K 10 8
♣ 7 4

When you lead the ace of diamonds East plays the knave and South the four. How should you continue?

That knave must be either singleton or doubleton and you can therefore give partner a diamond ruff. But are you sure that is a good idea? As well as the ruff partner will need the ace in one of the major suits if the contract is to be defeated. The danger is that if he has the ace of trumps it is quite likely to be a singleton. It would be a pity to telescope four defensive tricks into three by forcing partner to ruff a diamond with the singleton ace of trumps.

Since the declarer is marked with length in diamonds there is, no need to give partner a ruff on this hand. Your diamonds will be good for three tricks on their own. If the contract can be defeated at all, you will defeat it by switching to a trump. Partner may be able to win and shoot back a second diamond. And if partner has the ace of spades instead of the ace of hearts, the declarer will still be unable to score ten tricks unless he has a seventh heart or a spade void.

♠ 9 6 2
♡ A
◇ J 2
♣ J 9 8 6 5 3 2

♠ A 4
♡ K Q 9 7 4 3
◇ Q 5 4
♣ Q 10

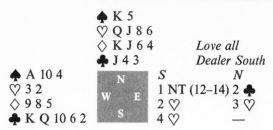

```
        ♠ K 5
        ♡ Q J 8 6
        ◇ K J 6 4        Love all
        ♣ J 4 3          Dealer South
♠ A 10 4
♡ 3 2            S              N
◇ 9 8 5          1 NT (12-14)   2 ♣
♣ K Q 10 6 2     2 ♡            3 ♡
                 4 ♡            —
```

On your lead of the king of clubs partner plays the seven and declarer the eight. How should you continue?

If partner has the ace of clubs, as seems likely, there is nothing to do but continue the suit and hope that partner can produce the fourth defensive trick in one of the red suits.

But there is also a chance that South is holding up with A x x in clubs. For this play to make sense South must be worried about a third-round club ruff which means he is unable to draw trumps immediately. If partner has the ace of trumps, any club continuation will suffice to defeat the contract. East will win the first round of trumps, lead a spade to your ace, and ruff the third round of clubs to take the setting trick.

However, partner could have the king of hearts and the ace of diamonds. To cater for this possibility as well as the others, you should continue with the queen of clubs at trick two. This will place the lead safely in the declarer's hand, and he will have to lead a spade or a diamond to gain access to dummy for a trump finesse. Whichever he chooses you will gain the lead in time to give partner his club ruff.

```
                        ♠ 9 8 6 3
                        ♡ K 7 5
                        ◇ A 10 7 2
                        ♣ 9 7
        ♠ Q J 7 2
        ♡ A 10 9 4
        ◇ Q 3
        ♣ A 8 5
```

9 · Anticipating a Discard Problem

There is nothing more agonizing than having to discard potential stoppers when the declarer runs his long suit, for it is never easy to be sure of doing the right thing. When you are in the grip of a genuine squeeze, for that matter, there will be no right thing to do. The agony can sometimes be averted, however, if at the moment when dummy goes down the defenders take the trouble to look ahead and see what is in store for them.

Certain basic conditions have to be fulfilled before any squeeze can operate. The declarer must have menaces in at least two suits, he must have adequate means of communication between his hand and dummy, and his timing must be right. On many hands it is quite impossible for the declarer to set up the position without the help of the defenders. Unfortunately, the required help is readily given. Faulty defence is the rule rather than the exception, and many a contract has been made on a squeeze that should never have arisen. The average defender tends to follow the course of least resistance, cashing every winner in sight and thereby tightening up a squeeze position against himself. It is those self-inflicted squeezes that are the most humiliating.

An effective defence will often suggest itself when the danger is recognized in time. A vital entry may be vulnerable to attack, or it may be possible to upset the timing by refusing to cash a winner. Even when no genuine squeeze can be on, there will be times when it is obvious that partner will have trouble with his discards if you cash too many winners. Try not to put him to the test if you have any reasonable alternative.

♠ Q 7 6 2
♡ 9 5
♢ A 7 2
♣ A 8 5 4

Love all
Dealer South

S	N
1 ♣	3 ♣
5 ♣	—

♠ 10 8 4 3
♡ K 8 6 3
♢ K Q 6
♣ K J

Partner leads the queen of hearts, you encourage with the eight and the declarer wins with the ace. A club is led to dummy's ace and a club returned to your king, West discarding the four of hearts on the second round. How should you continue?

Although fairly straightforward, this problem is a good test of defensive foresight. Do you see the danger ahead?

With five trump tricks and the two red aces, the declarer will need four spade tricks for his contract. If he has ace, king and knave of spades there is nothing you can do. But suppose that your partner has the knave of spades and the declarer the knave of diamonds. South would then have only ten tricks, but by cashing your king of hearts you would rectify his loser count and tighten up a spade-diamond squeeze against yourself. Clearly you must switch to the king of diamonds without cashing your heart winner. This will leave the declarer with two losers and no chance of a squeeze. In the end you will perhaps score a diamond and a spade instead of your heart trick.

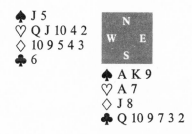

♠ J 5
♡ Q J 10 4 2
♢ 10 9 5 4 3
♣ 6

♠ A K 9
♡ A 7
♢ J 8
♣ Q 10 9 7 3 2

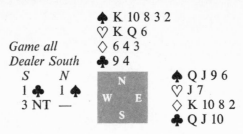

♠ K 10 8 3 2
♡ K Q 6
Game all ◇ 6 4 3
Dealer South ♣ 9 4

S	N
1 ♣	1 ♠
3 NT	—

♠ Q J 9 6
♡ J 7
◇ K 10 8 2
♣ Q J 10

Partner finds the lead of the queen of diamonds, on which you play the eight and South the five. West's knave of diamonds holds the next trick, but South wins the third round with the ace. After cashing the ace of spades, the declarer continues with the seven, on which your partner discards the three of hearts. Dummy plays low and you win with the nine. How do you continue?

On the bidding South is marked with the four aces and the king of clubs. Do you see what will happen if you cash the diamond winner at this point? No matter what you lead next, the declarer will win and cash three rounds of hearts, and you will have to part with a club and rely on partner having the eight.

There is no need to take such chances. The declarer is powerless to squeeze you on this hand. Only you can do it by cashing the winning diamond. If you refuse to do so, leading either a club or a spade instead, South will be able to make no more than eight tricks. On the third round of hearts you will discard the winning diamond, but you will thereafter score a trick in each of the black suits.

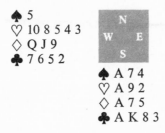

♠ 5
♡ 10 8 5 4 3
◇ Q J 9
♣ 7 6 5 2

♠ A 7 4
♡ A 9 2
◇ A 7 5
♣ A K 8 3

♠ J 7 6 2
♡ A Q 7
◇ K J 4   *Game all*
♣ 9 8 4   *Dealer West*

♠ A Q 10 9 3
♡ 9 5
◇ A 7 2
♣ Q J 5

W	N	E	S
1 ♠	—	—	1 NT
—	2 NT	—	3 NT
All pass			

You try the lead of the nine of hearts, which looks like a happy choice when partner drops the eight under dummy's ace. The declarer plays on diamonds and you allow the king and knave to win. East follows to the third round of diamonds as you capture South's ten with your ace. You lead the five of hearts on which dummy plays the seven, East the king and the declarer the ten. On the spade return South plays the king and you win with the ace. How do you continue?

Having only six points in the other suits, South is sure to possess the ace and king of clubs. If he also has the ten of clubs there is a danger that you might be squeezed in the black suits. By playing queen and another spade at this point you would rectify the timing for South. He would win with dummy's knave, cross to the king of clubs and cash the thirteenth diamond, on which you could spare the small spade. Dummy would discard a club, however, and the next lead of a heart to dummy's queen would fix you.

To avoid this fate you must lead the ten of spades without first cashing the queen.

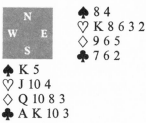

♠ 8 4
♡ K 8 6 3 2
◇ 9 6 5
♣ 7 6 2

♠ K 5
♡ J 10 4
◇ Q 10 8 3
♣ A K 10 3

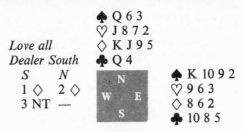

♠ Q 6 3
♡ J 8 7 2
◇ K J 9 5
♣ Q 4

Love all
Dealer South

♠ K 10 9 2
♡ 9 6 3
◇ 8 6 2
♣ 10 8 5

S	N
1 ◇	2 ◇
3 NT	—

On West's lead of the four of spades the three is played from dummy, you put in the nine and the declarer wins with the ace. South leads a diamond to the king and returns a diamond to his queen and West's ace. Partner continues with the five of spades and you capture the queen with your king, South following with the seven. How do you continue?

The defence has three spade tricks plus the ace of diamonds, but where is the setting trick to come from? Partner will need to have something good in clubs or hearts if the contract is to be defeated. A club trick can never run away, but if partner has the king of hearts there is a danger that he might be squeezed in hearts and clubs. You should therefore switch to the nine of hearts before cashing any more spades.

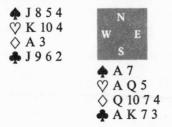

♠ J 8 5 4
♡ K 10 4
◇ A 3
♣ J 9 6 2

♠ A 7
♡ A Q 5
◇ Q 10 7 4
♣ A K 7 3

Note that it could be fatal to cash even one more round of spades before leading the heart. The declarer might then go up with the ace and play diamonds, catching West in a strip-squeeze. Partner would be forced to discard his last spade, enabling South to establish a second heart trick.

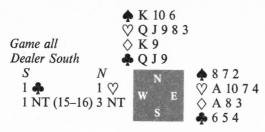

Game all
Dealer South

S	N
1 ♣	1 ♡
1 NT (15–16)	3 NT

West leads the five of diamonds against South's three no trump contract, and the nine is played from the table. How do you plan your defence?

Since partner cannot have more than five points, the only real hope is that his diamond lead is from a five-card suit headed by the queen. The natural thing to do is to win the first trick with the ace and return the eight of diamonds, but there is a hidden danger in this course. South may have five club tricks, in which case West will need to have a spade stopper if the contract is to be defeated. But on the run of the clubs partner will be able to keep his diamonds and his spade stopper only if he discards all his hearts. He may then be thrown in with a diamond and compelled to give the declarer his ninth trick in spades.

Provided that you maintain communication with partner, he will be able to discard all his hearts with impunity. At the first trick you should therefore play the eight of diamonds under dummy's nine.

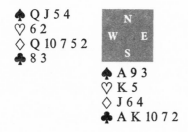

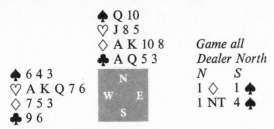

♠ Q 10
♡ J 8 5
◇ A K 10 8   *Game all*
♣ A Q 5 3   *Dealer North*

♠ 6 4 3   *N   S*
♡ A K Q 7 6   1 ◇   1 ♠
◇ 7 5 3   1 NT   4 ♠
♣ 9 6

You lead out the top hearts and partner discards the two of diamonds on the third round. How should you continue?

Assuming South to have no trump loser you can count nine top tricks, for he will certainly have a six-card suit on this bidding. It seems natural to switch to a club, but a little reflection will tell you that this would be short-sighted. The pressing need is to avert the danger of a minor suit squeeze against your partner.

It is a safe bet that the declarer has a singleton diamond, for partner would hardly have discarded one unless he had five cards in the suit. A diamond lead from you will therefore cut the declarer's communications and prevent any chance of a squeeze.

♠ 8 2
♡ 9 4
◇ Q J 9 6 2
♣ K J 7 4

♠ A K J 9 7 5
♡ 10 3 2
◇ 4
♣ 10 8 2

On a club switch the declarer would have put up the ace and run all the trumps to squeeze East in clubs and diamonds. Your partner should have seen the danger himself, of course. If he had been awake he would have saved you the problem by ruffing the third round of hearts and returning the queen of diamonds.

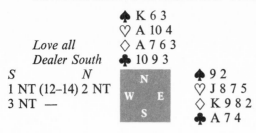

♠ K 6 3
♡ A 10 4
◇ A 7 6 3
♣ 10 9 3

Love all
Dealer South

♠ 9 2
♡ J 8 7 5
◇ K 9 8 2
♣ A 7 4

S	N
1 NT (12–14)	2 NT
3 NT	—

West leads the three of hearts, you cover dummy's four with the seven, and South wins with the queen. The diamond queen is run to your king, and you return a heart to the king and ace. When a diamond is led to South's knave, West discards the five of spades. The ten of diamonds is followed by a diamond to the ace, West discarding the nine of hearts and the two of clubs. The ten of hearts is then led to your knave, South discarding the four of spades. How do you continue?

The natural impulse to cash your fourth heart should be restrained. With six black cards left, West would have to abandon one of the suits on your heart lead and could easily do the wrong thing. There is no need to put him to the test, for your club ace ensures that you can cash the heart at a later stage. The four of clubs is your most attractive switch, although the nine of spades may do as well.

♠ Q 10 7 5
♡ K 9 6 3
◇ 5
♣ Q J 5 2

♠ A J 8 4
♡ Q 2
◇ Q J 10 4
♣ K 8 6

When the hand was played in the Junior European Championships at Dublin, East led the fourth heart on which South discarded a club. West had a tough decision to take and went wrong by letting go another spade.

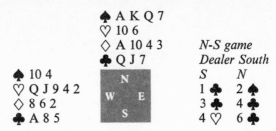

♠ A K Q 7
♡ 10 6
◇ A 10 4 3
♣ Q J 7

N-S game
Dealer South

♠ 10 4
♡ Q J 9 4 2
◇ 8 6 2
♣ A 8 5

S	N
1 ♣	2 ♠
3 ♣	4 ♣
4 ♡	6 ♣

On your lead of the queen of hearts partner plays the three and declarer the ace. East follows suit when a club is led to dummy's queen but discards the nine of diamonds on the next lead of the knave of clubs. How do you defend?

Although it is tempting to win and switch to a diamond in response to East's signal, this cannot be the right defence. An original diamond lead might have defeated the contract. Now it is too late. The declarer has five club tricks, three spades, two hearts and the ace of diamonds for a total of eleven tricks. There is hope for the defence only if East has the king of diamonds and a spade stopper, but a diamond switch will lead inevitably to a squeeze against East.

At this stage the only way to defeat the contract is to hold up the ace of trumps once more and then cut communications with a further heart lead. This prevents the declarer from bringing off his Vienna Coup and, with the diamond suit blocked, dummy is squeezed before East.

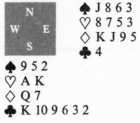

♠ J 8 6 3
♡ 8 7 5 3
◇ K J 9 5
♣ 4

♠ 9 5 2
♡ A K
◇ Q 7
♣ K 10 9 6 3 2

♠ 10 9 4
♡ K 8 7 5 3 2
◇ 7
♣ Q 7 5

Game all
Dealer South

♠ A Q
♡ Q 10 4
◇ 6 5 4 2
♣ A K J 6

S	N
1 ♠	2 ♠
4 ♠	—

Regrettably, West leads the queen of diamonds to the declarer's ace. South discards the five of clubs on the king of diamonds and continues with the ten of diamonds, covered by the knave and ruffed in dummy. The queen of clubs is then led to your king, South playing the four and West the two. How should you continue?

The play to the last trick seems to indicate that the declarer is hoping to ruff a club in dummy. You could stop the club ruff easily enough by playing the ace of spades followed by the queen, but that would by no means be a safe line of defence. Four trump tricks, the top diamonds and a diamond ruff plus the ace and king of hearts would give South nine tricks, and you might find yourself caught in a club-heart squeeze and forced to yield the tenth. The only way to prevent the club ruff *and* the squeeze is to lead the queen of spades without cashing the ace.

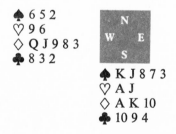

♠ 6 5 2
♡ 9 6
◇ Q J 9 8 3
♣ 8 3 2

♠ K J 8 7 3
♡ A J
◇ A K 10
♣ 10 9 4

The underlead in trumps retains control of the situation. You can win the next club lead, remove dummy's last trump with your ace, and cash another club to defeat the contract.

♠ A 7 6
♡ 8 6 3
◇ J 10 5   *E-W game*
♣ 8 7 4 3   *Dealer South*

♠ Q J 9 8
♡ A K Q J 5
◇ 3
♣ 6 5 2

S	W	N	E
1 ♠	2 ♡	2 ♠	4 ♡
4 ♠	Dbl.	All pass	

You start with top hearts and South ruffs the second round. He leads a spade to the ace, East following, and returns the knave of diamonds on which East plays the ace. South ruffs the heart return, cashes the king of spades and exits with the ten of spades to your knave, East discarding his last heart and the two of diamonds. How do you continue?

You can already count six tricks for the defence, but there is no law against trying for a seventh. That trick can come only from clubs, and it must be right to lead a club now rather than force partner to discard on your remaining hearts.

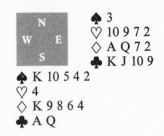

♠ 3
♡ 10 9 7 2
◇ A Q 7 2
♣ K J 10 9

♠ K 10 5 4 2
♡ 4
◇ K 9 8 6 4
♣ A Q

If you had cashed your hearts, East, discarding ahead of the declarer, would have had to throw two clubs. On your subsequent club lead South would have cashed ace and queen and led the king of diamonds. After ruffing, you would have had to yield the last trick to dummy's eight of clubs.

South's play was not the best, of course. He can do a couple of tricks better if he refrains from cashing the king of spades.

Note that it takes a double-dummy defence to defeat four hearts.

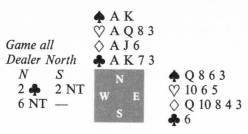

♠ A K
♡ A Q 8 3
♢ A J 6
♣ A K 7 3

Game all
Dealer North

N	S
2 ♣	2 NT
6 NT	—

♠ Q 8 6 3
♡ 10 6 5
♢ Q 10 8 4 3
♣ 6

Surprisingly, West leads the five of diamonds. The six is played from dummy, your ten draws the king, and South at once returns the suit. When West discards the two of clubs the ace is put on and the knave returned. How do you defend?

Presumably West had honour cards in the other three suits and chose the singleton lead as the least of evils. He can only have knaves, however, since the bidding marks South with the king of hearts and the queen of clubs. The declarer, therefore, has eleven tricks and the timing will be right for a club-heart squeeze against West if you win this trick. Is there anything you can do about it? Yes, you can force South to play his squeeze card too early by returning a diamond. West has idle cards in spades at this stage and dummy will be squeezed first.

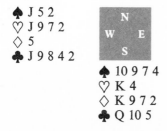

♠ J 5 2
♡ J 9 7 2
♢ 5
♣ J 9 8 4 2

♠ 10 9 7 4
♡ K 4
♢ K 9 7 2
♣ Q 10 5

If you return anything but a diamond, South will win on the table, play off the ace and king of spades, return to hand with the king of hearts and lead the diamond to finish West off. Note that it would not do for you to duck the knave of diamonds, for then the declarer would eventually throw West in with the fourth heart to compel a fatal club lead.

♠ 6 4 2
♡ A K 3
♦ K 10 5
♣ A 10 8 4

Game all
Dealer North

♠ A K 5
♡ Q 9 2
♦ 4 3
♣ K J 9 7 6

N	S
1 ♣	1 ♦
1 NT	3 ♦
3 ♡	5 ♦

Partner leads the seven of spades and the declarer plays the nine under your king. How should you continue?

Everything points to the seven of spades being a normal fourth-highest lead, in which case South's remaining high spade will be the knave, not the queen. With a sequence headed by J 10 8 West would have led the knave rather than the seven. Where is the setting trick to come from? South is not likely to have a third spade. But on the bidding it sounds as though he has no more than seven diamonds, so there should be a third trick for the defence somewhere.

If South has a doubleton club you must always make a club trick. The dangerous situation is where South has a singleton club and three hearts headed by the knave. Then he will have a ruffing squeeze against you in hearts and clubs. What can you do about it? Nothing from your side of the table, for a heart lead would permit South to score the knave. A heart lead from partner would do the trick, though. You should therefore return the five of spades at trick two and hope that partner can work it out.

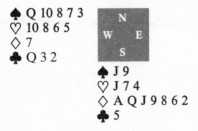

♠ Q 10 8 7 3
♡ 10 8 6 5
♦ 7
♣ Q 3 2

♠ J 9
♡ J 7 4
♦ A Q J 9 8 6 2
♣ 5

♠ 7 6
♡ J 9 5 2
◇ A Q 8 4
♣ A K 7

Love all
Dealer South

♠ A 3
♡ A K Q 7
◇ 6 5 2
♣ Q 10 8 3

S	N
3 ♠	4 ♠

You start with the ace and king of hearts, partner following with the three and six and declarer with the four and eight. How should you continue?

It is clear that partner has the ten of hearts since he failed to echo. The setting trick will have to come from one of the minor suits, and there is a temptation to switch to a diamond at trick three. That would be both unwise and unnecessary, however. If partner has a diamond trick he must make it in due course. Your urgent task is to protect yourself against a heart-club squeeze, and you can do that only by continuing with the queen of hearts.

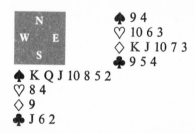

♠ 9 4
♡ 10 6 3
◇ K J 10 7 3
♣ 9 5 4

♠ K Q J 10 8 5 2
♡ 8 4
◇ 9
♣ J 6 2

The declarer will ruff the third heart and lead a trump, but you will win immediately and continue with a fourth round of hearts to wipe out the menace. You will then have nothing but clubs to look after, and with partner taking care of the diamonds, the declarer will have no further play for his contract.

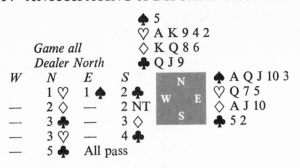

```
                    ♠ 5
                    ♡ A K 9 4 2
      Game all      ◇ K Q 8 6
      Dealer North  ♣ Q J 9
  W    N    E    S                  ♠ A Q J 10 3
       1♡   1♠   2♣                 ♡ Q 7 5
  —    2◇   —    2 NT               ◇ A J 10
  —    3♣   —    3◇                 ♣ 5 2
  —    3♡   —    4♣
  —    5♣  All pass
```

West leads the nine of spades and you win the trick with the
ace. How should you continue?

South is marked with a five-card club suit. Assuming he has no
trump loser, the defence will have a chance only if his distribution
is precisely 3-1-4-5. If South has two hearts, for instance, he will
be able to establish the heart suit without difficulty, and if he has
four spades he will either ruff two losing spades in dummy, set up
a long heart trick, or squeeze you in spades and diamonds, according to how you defend.

With a 3-1-4-5 shape, South will have five trump tricks, the
king of spades and a spade ruff, two hearts and one diamond for
a total of ten tricks. Could he establish the fifth heart in dummy
as his eleventh trick? At first glance it seems impossible. By the
time he has ruffed two hearts and drawn trumps he will have no
trumps left, and by keeping a spade with your ace of diamonds
you should be able to defeat the contract when a diamond is led.

But that analysis does not take account of your own discard
problem. Suppose you return a trump. The declarer will win in
dummy, cash the top hearts and ruff a heart, ruff his small spade,
ruff another heart and draw the last two trumps. With two
discards to find, you will be in trouble. If you part with two
spades, South will lead the king of spades to extract your last
card in the suit and a diamond lead will give him eventual access

to the winning heart on the table. If you let go a diamond, South will be able to abandon the king of spades in his hand and rely on making a second diamond trick instead.

The only way to prevent the declarer from establishing and enjoying the fifth heart is to attack the outside entry in dummy. You should therefore lead the knave of diamonds at trick two.

The full hand:

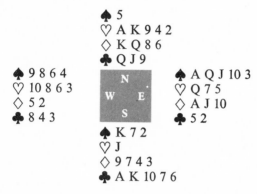

```
                    ♠ 5
                    ♡ A K 9 4 2
                    ◇ K Q 8 6
                    ♣ Q J 9
  ♠ 9 8 6 4                        ♠ A Q J 10 3
  ♡ 10 8 6 3                       ♡ Q 7 5
  ◇ 5 2                            ◇ A J 10
  ♣ 8 4 3                          ♣ 5 2
                    ♠ K 7 2
                    ♡ J
                    ◇ 9 7 4 3
                    ♣ A K 10 7 6
```

10 · Working from First Principles

Most of our defensive errors are brought about by a superficial analysis that fails to take into account some vital piece of data. We make certain assumptions that seem reasonable at the time and hasten to act on them without checking their validity. What we ought to do after reaching a tentative conclusion is to test it against all the known facts and see if it still stands up. We should ask ourselves constantly if there is anything at all in the bidding or in the play, so far, that does not accord with our general view of the situation.

This involves going back to first principles—counting the declarer's points, counting his distribution, counting his tricks, and reviewing every available inference. Paying due regard to the line of play adopted by the declarer, we must ask ourselves how he plans to make his contract and how he might conceivably be thwarted. Often there will be just one possible answer.

Defence is predominately an exercise in logic. 'Once the impossible has been eliminated,' as the great detective was fond of saying, 'what remains, however improbable, must be the truth.' There are few defensive problems that do not lend themselves to this approach. A defender who goes astray towards the end of a hand may complain that there was nothing to guide him, but you can lay long odds that he has missed a sitting inference. Almost invariably there will be clues from the bidding and the play which will enable you to eliminate all lines of defence but the winning one.

♠ 9 6 3
♡ 9 8 6 2
Game all ◊ K Q 10 5
Dealer South ♣ 7 5

S	N
1 ♡	2 ♡
4 ♡	—

♠ Q 10 8 2
♡ 10 7 3
◊ A 7 6
♣ A 9 4

When West leads the king of clubs you encourage with the nine and South plays the six. Partner continues with the three of clubs, and the declarer plays the knave under your ace. How should you continue?

Since you have no more than three tricks in the minor suits it is clear that the setting trick will have to come either from trumps or from spades, with the latter the better bet. But there is no need for haste in attacking spades. There is a much more pressing job to be done first.

The clue is in your partner's lead of the three of clubs, which tells you that the declarer has another card in the suit in spite of his play of the knave. You should therefore give the declarer his club ruff immediately so as to take out dummy's trump entry and kill the diamond suit.

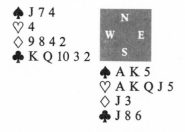

♠ J 7 4
♡ 4
◊ 9 8 4 2
♣ K Q 10 3 2

♠ A K 5
♡ A K Q J 5
◊ J 3
♣ J 8 6

After your club return the declarer will eventually attack diamonds, whether he draws trumps first or not. But your partner's echo will tell you to take the ace of diamonds on the second round and you will make your spade trick in due course.

♠ 8 7 2
♡ J 10 3
◇ 7 5   *Game all*
♣ A K J 9 5   *Dealer South*

♠ K J 4
♡ A Q 6   S   N
◇ Q J 9   1 ♡   2 ♣
♣ 10 7 6 3   2 NT (15–16) 3 ♡
                         3 NT

On your lead of the queen of diamonds partner plays the eight and declarer the two. You continue with the knave of diamonds, East playing the four and South the ten. What now?

This is a simple matter of counting points. Partner is marked with the king of diamonds, and South must have every other face card to justify his two no trump rebid. Clearly a diamond continuation is pointless and will waste a valuable tempo. Given time, South will establish two heart tricks which, with five clubs and two aces, will be enough for his contract.

The only hope is that partner has the ten of spades, in which case you will be able to set up a fifth trick for the defence before the declarer can set up his ninth. You should therefore switch immediately to the king or knave of spades.

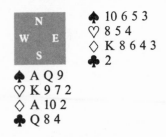

♠ 10 6 5 3
♡ 8 5 4
◇ K 8 6 4 3
♣ 2

♠ A Q 9
♡ K 9 7 2
◇ A 10 2
♣ Q 8 4

Note that it would not be good enough to switch to the four of spades. The declarer would then cash his eight winners and throw you in with the third round of spades to lead away from your ace of hearts. You have to unblock twice to enable partner to win the third round of spades.

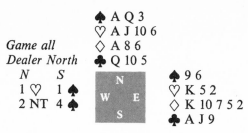

Game all
Dealer North

N	S
1 ♡	1 ♠
2 NT	4 ♠

♠ A Q 3
♡ A J 10 6
◇ A 8 6
♣ Q 10 5

♠ 9 6
♡ K 5 2
◇ K 10 7 5 2
♣ A J 9

West leads the four of clubs, the ten is played from dummy, and South plays the two under your knave. How should you continue?

There will be nothing much to worry about if you can score three club tricks, since one of your red kings is likely to be worth a trick. But if South has only two clubs the prospects are not so good, for you will then need a trick in both hearts and diamonds. To continue with the ace and another club will not do. South might then be able to get the hearts going for a diamond discard.

A diamond lead from your side of the table would be too risky since declarer might well have the queen. What you need is a diamond lead from partner, and you can achieve that only if you return the nine of clubs at trick two.

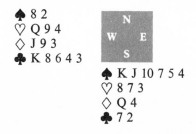

♠ 8 2
♡ Q 9 4
◇ J 9 3
♣ K 8 6 4 3

♠ K J 10 7 5 4
♡ 8 7 3
◇ Q 4
♣ 7 2

When partner wins the second trick with the king of clubs it will not be hard for him to work out what is needed.

On the lie of the cards, three no trumps by North would have been a happier contract.

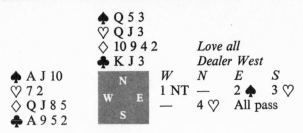

♠ Q 5 3
♡ Q J 3
◇ 10 9 4 2   *Love all*
♣ K J 3   *Dealer West*

♠ A J 10
♡ 7 2
◇ Q J 8 5
♣ A 9 5 2

W	N	E	S
1 NT	—	2 ♠	3 ♡
—	4 ♡	All pass	

You lead the ace of spades and continue with the knave when East encourages. South ruffs the second spade and leads the eight of clubs. How do you defend?

Since partner is not likely to have a trump trick, you will need three tricks from the minor suits. There is no point in playing low on the first club, for in view of your no trump opening the declarer will not misguess the position. If you do play low there is a serious risk that you will find yourself short of exit cards at a later stage. You should therefore take the ace of clubs and return the suit.

♠ K 9 8 6 4 2
♡ K 5
◇ 6
♣ Q 10 7 6

♠ 7
♡ A 10 9 8 6 4
◇ A K 7 3
♣ 8 4

Had you played low on the club lead the declarer would have won with the king, drawn trumps, ruffed dummy's last spade, cashed a top diamond and led another club. No matter which defender won the trick the only safe return would have been a club, but South would have ruffed and played a small diamond to hold his losers to three tricks.

Your play of the ace and another club breaks up the elimination by removing an exit card from South's hand.

♠ A K 8 4
♡ K 10
◇ 10 5 3
♣ A J 10 6

Game all
Dealer North

N	S
1 ♣	1 ♠
3 ♠	4 ♠

♠ Q 6 3
♡ J 7 4 2
◇ K Q 8 4
♣ 7 3

West leads the three of hearts, you cover the ten with your knave, and South wins with the ace. Two rounds of trumps are drawn with the ace and king, partner following with the five and the knave. Then the six of clubs is led to South's king, a club returned to dummy's ace and the knave of clubs led from the table. How do you defend?

In addition to your trump trick, you will need three diamonds to defeat the contract, so you must rely on partner for the ace. A count of declarer's distribution will keep you straight. From the bidding and the early play you know that South began with four spades and three hearts. If he has only two clubs, as seems likely on this line of play, he will have four diamonds and a discard will not help him.

You should therefore ruff with your master trump just in case South is up to some trickery.

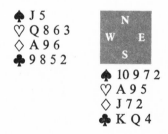

♠ J 5
♡ Q 8 6 3
◇ A 9 6
♣ 9 8 5 2

♠ 10 9 7 2
♡ A 9 5
◇ J 7 2
♣ K Q 4

Note what happens if you fail to ruff. The queen wins and South returns to dummy with the king of hearts to lead the ten of clubs. This time he does get rid of a loser whether you ruff or not.

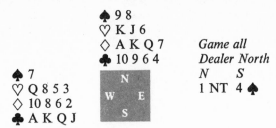

♠ 9 8
♡ K J 6
◊ A K Q 7   *Game all*
♣ 10 9 6 4   *Dealer North*

♠ 7   *N   S*
♡ Q 8 5 3   1 NT   4 ♠
◊ 10 8 6 2
♣ A K Q J

There is no problem with the opening lead on this hand. You start with top clubs and East discards the two of hearts on the third round. How should you continue?

At a casual glance it may seem harmless to continue with the fourth club, but this is a situation that calls for another hard look. The setting trick can come only from trumps, and partner may have the type of stopper that can be picked up by a trump coup. It is up to you to protect that hypothetical stopper in every way you can.

Holding six trumps, the declarer would have to ruff twice in his hand before he could bring off a trump coup. A club continuation would help him by shortening his trumps immediately. A diamond switch would also be unsafe, for South might then be able to ruff two diamonds in hand, using the king and knave of hearts as the entries to get back to dummy. It is a heart switch that is required at trick four, for that will take out one of dummy's entries prematurely.

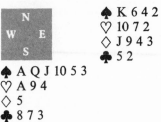

♠ K 6 4 2
♡ 10 7 2
◊ J 9 4 3
♣ 5 2

♠ A Q J 10 5 3
♡ A 9 4
◊ 5
♣ 8 7 3

The heart lead leaves the declarer with no further play for his contract when the trumps fail to break evenly.

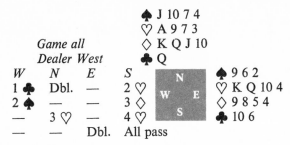

♠ J 10 7 4
♡ A 9 7 3
◇ K Q J 10
♣ Q

Game all
Dealer West

♠ 9 6 2
♡ K Q 10 4
◇ 9 8 5 4
♣ 10 6

W	N	E	S
1 ♣	Dbl.	—	2 ♡
2 ♠	—	—	3 ◇
—	3 ♡	—	4 ♡
—	—	Dbl.	All pass

After leading the ace of spades West switches to the two of trumps. The three is played from dummy and your queen wins the trick. How do you justify your double?

On the bidding the distribution is plain enough. Partner is 6-5 in the black suits with two red singletons, and the declarer has a 1-4-4-4 shape. Now count the declarer's tricks. If you allow him the minor suit aces, he has four diamonds and one club and will need five tricks from trumps to make his contract. Has he a chance of making five trump tricks? Certainly, if you don't return a trump at trick three. The ace of trumps plus one club ruff in dummy and three spade ruffs in hand will see him home.

You must, therefore, return a trump, but the lead of a small trump will not be good enough. That would enable South to score two trump tricks plus three ruffs. The only way to defeat this contract is to return the king of hearts at trick three. The declarer will then be unable to ruff two spades without establishing your ten of hearts and will make no more than nine tricks.

♠ A K Q 8 5
♡ 2
◇ 7
♣ K J 9 5 3 2

♠ 3
♡ J 8 6 5
◇ A 6 3 2
♣ A 8 7 4

♠ K Q 9
♡ A K Q J 7   *Love all*
◇ 7 6   *Dealer South*
♣ 8 5 4

♠ 6
♡ 10 8 5 4 2
◇ K J 8 3
♣ K Q 10

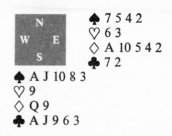

S	N
1 ♣	2 ♡
2 ♠	3 ♡
3 ♠	4 ♠

On your lead of the three of diamonds partner plays the ace and declarer the nine. East returns the four of diamonds and you capture South's queen with your king. What now?

The king of clubs may try to jump out of your hand, but you should hold it back while you review the situation. The declarer must surely have five cards headed by the ace and knave in each of the black suits, in which case a club lead will serve no purpose. South would simply win with the ace, draw trumps and claim ten tricks. In fact, if he took the trouble to cash his fifth trump, he would make eleven tricks, for you would be squeezed in clubs and hearts.

On this hand the way to give the declarer a headache is to cut his link with dummy by leading a heart. Partner's four trumps will be an embarrassment to South. After two rounds of trumps he will have to run the hearts, but partner will ruff one of the winners and South will be unable to score more than nine tricks.

If you lead a small heart South is unlikely to run it, but there is no point in taking chances. Just in case South's singleton is the nine, you should lead the ten of hearts.

♠ 7 5 4 2
♡ 6 3
◇ A 10 5 4 2
♣ 7 2

♠ A J 10 8 3
♡ 9
◇ Q 9
♣ A J 9 6 3

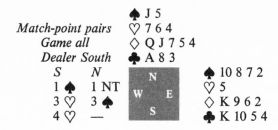

Match-point pairs
Game all
Dealer South

♠ J 5
♡ 7 6 4
◇ Q J 7 5 4
♣ A 8 3

♠ 10 8 7 2
♡ 5
◇ K 9 6 2
♣ K 10 5 4

S	N
1 ♠	1 NT
3 ♡	3 ♠
4 ♡	—

West leads the two of clubs, the three is played from dummy and you win with the king. How should you continue?

To have ducked in dummy, the declarer must surely have the queen and another club, and since he is marked with five cards in each major suit, he can have only one diamond. If it is a loser, South may be able to discard it on the ace of clubs, and you should, therefore, switch to diamonds at once. But any diamond will not do. To give yourself a chance of defeating the contract you must lead the king. West is marked with four trumps, and if these include a top honour your lead of the king and another diamond will cause the declarer to lose trump control. After winning his trump trick, partner will be able to establish a second trump winner for himself by leading the ace of diamonds.

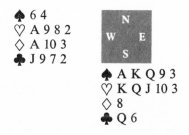

♠ 6 4
♡ A 9 8 2
◇ A 10 3
♣ J 9 7 2

♠ A K Q 9 3
♡ K Q J 10 3
◇ 8
♣ Q 6

South could have made sure of his contract by winning the first club and leading a trump, but at pairs the chance of an overtrick was too great a temptation for him.

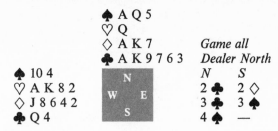

♠ A Q 5
♡ Q
◇ A K 7   *Game all*
♣ A K 9 7 6 3   *Dealer North*

♠ 10 4
♡ A K 8 2
◇ J 8 6 4 2
♣ Q 4

N	S
2 ♣	2 ◇
3 ♣	3 ♠
4 ♠	—

On your lead of the ace of hearts partner plays the knave and declarer the three. How should you continue?

The knave of hearts might be interpreted as a suit-preference signal, but it is hard to imagine a hand on which partner would want a diamond switch. More likely, East is showing solid hearts. Since partner will need to have a couple of trump tricks to give the defence a chance, there is a temptation to switch to trumps in order to cut down heart ruffs. But a little thought should tell you that South does not need heart ruffs to make his contract. All he need do is bring in dummy's club suit, and a trump lead would actually help him to keep control of the hand.

The one way in which you might cause the declarer to lose control is by forcing dummy. You should therefore continue with a small heart at trick two.

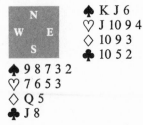

♠ K J 6
♡ J 10 9 4
◇ 10 9 3
♣ 10 5 2

♠ 9 8 7 3 2
♡ 7 6 5 3
◇ Q 5
♣ J 8

On the heart continuation the declarer is unable to draw trumps, yet he cannot dispose of all his heart losers without allowing the defenders to make three trump tricks. In a Crockfords Cup final some years ago, however, the winning defence was not found.

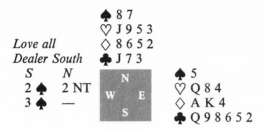

♠ 8 7
♡ J 9 5 3
◇ 8 6 5 2
♣ J 7 3

Love all
Dealer South

S	N
2 ♠	2 NT
3 ♠	—

♠ 5
♡ Q 8 4
◇ A K 4
♣ Q 9 8 6 5 2

West leads the knave of diamonds and South drops the queen under your king. How should you continue?

At this stage you know very little about the declarer's hand, but a switch to either hearts or clubs is clearly too dangerous to contemplate. The queen of diamonds may not be a singleton, of course, and it seems natural to continue with the ace of diamonds in order to clarify the position. But that course also has its dangers. If the declarer has no more diamonds you will have wasted an exit card which may be sorely missed in the end game. There is no real need for a diamond continuation, for if South has another losing diamond he will have no means of disposing of it. You should therefore play safe by switching to your trump at trick two.

♠ Q 9 3
♡ 10 6 2
◇ J 10 9 7 3
♣ A 10

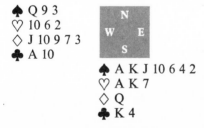

♠ A K J 10 6 4 2
♡ A K 7
◇ Q
♣ K 4

The declarer will probably play ace, king and another trump, and West will have no safe return but a diamond. South will ruff and continue with ace, king and another heart. On winning the queen, however, you will still have an exit card in your third diamond, and the declarer will eventually have to lead clubs himself.

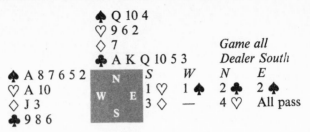

	S	W	N	E
	1 ♡	1 ♠	2 ♣	2 ♠
	3 ♢	—	4 ♡	All pass

On your lead of the ace of spades partner plays the nine and declarer the three. How should you continue?

There can hardly be a second spade trick for the defence, and on the bidding the declarer is likely to have the ace of diamonds. In that case you will need three tricks from trumps to defeat the contract. The only line of defence that holds out any promise is an attack on communications, and you should therefore switch to a club at trick two. You can lead a second club when in with the ace of hearts and the declarer may have to work hard for his contract.

When South wins the second club in dummy he will have a choice of plays. The winning line is to continue with a third club, banking on the defender with the doubleton club to have three hearts. But South may decide to play for a 4-3 diamond break, leading a diamond to his ace, ruffing a diamond, ruffing a spade and attempting to ruff another diamond. If South adopts this line he will go down, for you will ruff the third diamond ahead of dummy and partner's trumps will be good for the setting trick.

Note that South has an easy ride on any other defence.

```
                    ♠ A Q 10 9 3
                    ♡ J 8 3
                    ◇ K               N-S game
                    ♣ A J 10 5        Dealer South
    ♠ 8 7 4         ┌─────────┐      S     N
    ♡ 2             │    N    │      1 ♡   1 ♠
    ◇ A J 8 4 3     │ W     E │      2 ◇   3 ♣
    ♣ Q 8 4 2       │    S    │      3 ◇   5 ♡
                    └─────────┘      6 ♡   —
```

Your lead of the eight of spades goes to the declarer's king and a small diamond is led. You take the ace and return a low diamond which is ruffed in dummy with the three of hearts while partner follows suit with the ten. On the lead of the knave of hearts East plays the four and South the six. Next comes the eight of hearts, East playing the five and South the nine. The declarer then leads the six of clubs from hand. How do you defend?

This sort of problem tends to be rather easier on paper than it is at the table. From the fact that the declarer has stopped drawing trumps you can deduce that partner has the guarded king in his hand. South is seeking an extra entry to dummy in order that he may reduce his trumps to the same number as East's and bring off a trump coup. You must, of course, put up the queen of clubs to deny him the extra entry.

```
          ┌─────────┐    ♠ J 6 5 2
          │    N    │    ♡ K 7 5 4
          │ W     E │    ◇ 10 5
          │    S    │    ♣ 9 7 3
          └─────────┘
          ♠ K
          ♡ A Q 10 9 6
          ◇ Q 9 7 6 2
          ♣ K 6
```

If you had played low on the club lead, the declarer would have finessed dummy's knave, ruffed a spade and returned to the table by overtaking the king of clubs. The run of the spades would then have enabled him to discard his diamonds, and pick up the outstanding trumps.

Your chance to defeat the contract came through imprecise play on the declarer's part. South should have played the trumps from dummy in reverse order, first the eight and then the knave. When the bad trump break showed up the lead would have been in dummy, where it was needed, and South would have had no trouble in bringing off his trump coup.

11 • Discarding to Deceive

The true calibre of a defender can be measured by his reactions when he finds himself with his back to the wall, fighting in what appears to be a hopeless cause. We all know defenders who lose interest in the proceedings as soon as it becomes clear that the declarer can make his contract. Pained at being involved in such a boring business, they play out their remaining cards in a routine fashion with a minimum of thought, hoping only for better luck on the next hand. This is the attitude of the born loser.

The resourceful defender does not give in so easily. Although acknowledging that the contract can be made, he continues to fight an energetic rearguard action until the last card has been played, for he realizes that what is obvious to him may be far from obvious to the declarer. In such situations a deceptive discard may be all that is needed to give the declarer a false picture of the distribution and set him on the wrong road.

Deceptive discarding can earn big rewards in the end game, especially in throw-in situations. The expert defender has a rooted objection to being thrown in to make a fatal lead from an honour card. He regards this as the ultimate indignity and rarely permits it to happen. Instead he elects to bare his honour card, so that the declarer has to guess between finessing, playing for the drop, or attempting a throw-in. Inevitably the declarer will guess wrong some of the time, thereby losing a contract that would have been made against a defender who followed the course of least resistance.

The practice of unguarding honour cards is not as dangerous as it might appear, for unless the declarer has an accurate count on the hand he has no means of knowing what has happened. As with any deceptive manœuvre, of course, the baring of honour cards must be done in a natural manner and without a tell-tale trance. The key discard should be made at an early stage rather than at the last moment.

In squeeze endings deceptive discarding can again be of value. A defender in the grip of a fully-established squeeze may not be completely helpless. Many squeeze endings are full of ambiguity when the declarer has been unable to obtain a count of the hand. In such cases it may be possible by means of your discards to persuade the declarer that you have abandoned a suit which in fact you still hold. On other hands you may be able to put up a convincing pretence of being squeezed where no squeeze exists, and thus lead the declarer to his doom.

The chance of success of such artistic defence will naturally depend very much on the stature of your opponent. There are not so many declarers who are good enough to be deceived in this manner. Those without imagination will stolidly play the cards in front of them and make their contracts in spite of your best efforts.

Fortunately, it is not only in squeeze and throw-in situations that deceptive discarding can be effective, and it is not only against first-class declarers that it is worth trying. There are many common situations where the obvious choice of discard will be a mistake, not because it gives a trick away in itself but because it provides a significant clue that may guide the declarer to the winning play. In bridge it often pays to do the unexpected thing. An off-beat decision to part freely with your assets and hang grimly on to a suit in which your holding is quite worthless may work out surprisingly well. A slightly unorthodox choice of discard may be all that is needed to throw the declarer off balance.

```
                        ♠ A Q 4
                        ♡ A K Q 8
                        ◇ 9 6 3
        Love all        ♣ K 6 3
        Dealer East
    W    N    E    S              ♠ K 5
              1 NT  —             ♡ J 9 6 2
    2 ◇  Dbl.  —   3 ♣            ◇ A K 8 4
     —   4 ♣   —   5 ♣            ♣ Q 7 4
    All pass
```

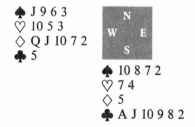

You overtake West's queen of diamonds with the king and continue with the ace which South ruffs. West follows suit when a
small club is led to the king, but discards the three of hearts when
the knave of clubs is finessed on the way back. He discards the
five of hearts on the ace of clubs, and throws the two of diamonds
when a fourth club is led. The four of spades is thrown from
dummy. What do you discard?

The declarer has six club tricks, three hearts and the ace of
spades, and it is clear that he can make his eleventh trick by
throwing you in with the fourth heart to lead into the spade
tenace. To avoid this indignity and make South guess, you must
discard the five of spades on this trick.

```
    ♠ J 9 6 3
    ♡ 10 5 3
    ◇ Q J 10 7 2
    ♣ 5
                        ♠ 10 8 7 2
                        ♡ 7 4
                        ◇ 5
                        ♣ A J 10 9 8 2
```

After your spade discard South may go astray by playing you
for a 3-4-3-3 distribution and throwing you in with the fourth
heart. Note that it would not be good enough to discard a diamond on the fourth trump, intending to throw your small spade
next time. The next time might never come, for South could enter
dummy in hearts and ruff out the last diamond to obtain a complete
blueprint of your distribution.

♠ Q 9 5
♡ K 9 2
◇ A Q 7 5   *Love all*
♣ 10 8 3   *Dealer South*

♠ 6 2   *S   N*
♡ J 8 7 4 3   1 ♠   2 NT
◇ J 10 6 3   3 ♡   4 ♠
♠ J 2

Your lead of the knave of clubs holds the trick, East playing
the seven and South the four. You continue with the two of clubs
to East's queen and South's ace. When the declarer leads a low
spade to the queen, partner produces the ace and cashes the king
of clubs. What do you discard?

You must be careful not to simplify the play for the declarer
here. South is likely to have a 5-4-1-3 distribution and he will
discover soon enough that you started with only two trumps. A
heart discard would be a complete giveaway. South would know
that you must have five, for under no circumstances would you
discard from four hearts when you had five diamonds. After
cashing the ace of hearts, South would have a simple finesse
against your knave for his contract.

You should therefore discard a diamond.

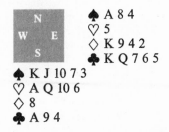

♠ A 8 4
♡ 5
◇ K 9 4 2
♣ K Q 7 6 5

♠ K J 10 7 3
♡ A Q 10 6
◇ 8
♣ A 9 4

East will presumably switch back to trumps and South will
have a chance of getting it wrong. If he places you with five diamonds and four hearts he may cash the diamond ace, ruff a diamond high, enter dummy in trumps while you discard a heart,
and ruff another diamond. When the king fails to fall he may
decide that you were squeezed on the third round of trumps and
try to drop the knave of hearts.

It is often a mistake to discard the 'useless' fifth card in a suit, if only because it makes it easy for the declarer to count the hand.

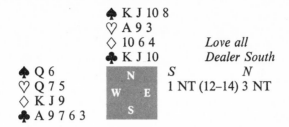

♠ K J 10 8
♡ A 9 3
◇ 10 6 4   *Love all*
♣ K J 10   *Dealer South*

♠ Q 6
♡ Q 7 5
◇ K J 9
♣ A 9 7 6 3

S	N
1 NT (12–14)	3 NT

South wins your club lead with the queen and runs the nine of spades to East's ace. Partner returns a club and you play the ace and another, East discarding the two of hearts on the third round. South leads a diamond to his ace and continues spades, capturing your queen with dummy's king. After following to the next spade, the declarer discards a diamond on the fourth round. What are your two discards?

The declarer needs the outstanding face-cards for his bid, and it is clear that he can make nine tricks if he reads the position correctly. Since to keep three hearts is bound to be fatal, a heart should be your first discard. What about the other one? A discard of the knave of diamonds is unlikely to work, for South will play off the king and ace of hearts before trying a diamond from dummy. A better idea is to let go a club. South will not expect you to discard a winning club if you have any spare diamonds in your hand, and he may well lead a diamond next, playing you for an original holding of four hearts and king and another diamond.

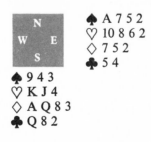

♠ A 7 5 2
♡ 10 8 6 2
◇ 7 5 2
♣ 5 4

♠ 9 4 3
♡ K J 4
◇ A Q 8 3
♣ Q 8 2

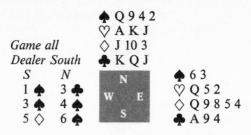

```
                    ♠ Q 9 4 2
                    ♡ A K J
   Game all         ◇ J 10 3
   Dealer South     ♣ K Q J
     S     N                      ♠ 6 3
     1 ♠   3 ♣                    ♡ Q 5 2
     3 ♠   4 ♠                    ◇ Q 9 8 5 4
     5 ◇   6 ♠                    ♣ A 9 4
```

West leads the nine of hearts and dummy's ace wins the trick. All follow to the ace and king of trumps, and the declarer leads a club next. You take the ace and return the suit, and after cashing the third round of clubs, the declarer leads the knave of diamonds from the table. You play low, South wins with the ace, and West follows with the two. Then comes a low trump on which your partner discards the thirteenth club. Plan your discards.

On the play, it seems certain that South started with doubleton ace and king of diamonds and three hearts headed by the ten. Although he has only eleven top tricks, he will discard dummy's knave of hearts on the last spade to catch you in a criss-cross squeeze. Since he has to retain top cards in two suits, however, the position is ambiguous and you may yet escape with your skin. If you discard three diamonds, South will hardly be able to avoid doing the right thing. He will probably also get it right if you discard two diamonds and then a heart. The best chance is to throw the heart first and follow with the five and nine of diamonds. South may then go wrong by cashing his ace of diamonds next.

```
     ♠ 8 5
     ♡ 9 8 7 3
     ◇ 7 6 2
     ♣ 8 7 5 2
```

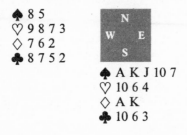

```
                    ♠ A K J 10 7
                    ♡ 10 6 4
                    ◇ A K
                    ♣ 10 6 3
```

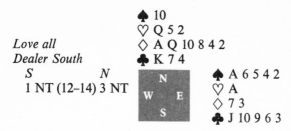

Love all
Dealer South

♠ 10	
♡ Q 5 2	
◇ A Q 10 8 4 2	
♣ K 7 4	

S   N
1 NT (12–14) 3 NT

♠ A 6 5 4 2
♡ A
◇ 7 3
♣ J 10 9 6 3

On this hand you know which suit partner is going to lead before his knave of hearts hits the table. The two is played from dummy and South drops the three under your ace. You try a switch to the knave of clubs, which produces the five from South, the queen from West and the king from dummy. A small diamond is led from the table and, surprisingly, the declarer plays the nine. Your partner wins with the knave and returns the two of clubs to your nine and South's ace. The declarer's next move is to lead the king of diamonds and overtake with dummy's ace. Plan your discards on the diamonds.

To play in this manner South must be certain of nine tricks. No doubt he has the kings of both spades and hearts, and his safety-play in diamonds was dictated by fear of a spade lead from your hand. Such a careful declarer is perhaps unlikely to play himself down, but you have nothing to lose by offering him an opportunity. The only hope is to create the illusion that he can make an easy overtrick. If South has a tenace position in hearts and can be persuaded that your partner has the ace of spades, he may think it safe to recover the trick he lost in diamonds by throwing your partner on lead at the end.

But how can you convince the declarer that your partner has the ace of spades? It is not such an impossible task. All you have to do is discard a couple of winners. On the run of the diamonds you should throw only two small spades plus two winning clubs. Such a sequence of discards would be compatible with an original holding in spades of five cards headed by the queen. More to the point, in the declarer's mind it will be incompatible with a holding of five cards headed by the ace. Players who possess a sure outside entry do not normally discard winners.

The full hand:

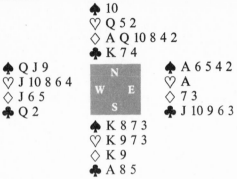

```
              ♠ 10
              ♡ Q 5 2
              ◇ A Q 10 8 4 2
              ♣ K 7 4
♠ Q J 9                        ♠ A 6 5 4 2
♡ J 10 8 6 4                   ♡ A
◇ J 6 5                        ◇ 7 3
♣ Q 2                          ♣ J 10 9 6 3
              ♠ K 8 7 3
              ♡ K 9 7 3
              ◇ K 9
              ♣ A 8 5
```

On the run of the diamonds West will perforce discard a heart and the nine and knave of spades, while South throws the three small spades. When the queen of hearts is led from dummy you will throw another small spade, and the declarer, if he fancies his card-reading, will be very tempted to lead a spade next for the overtrick.

Mind you, if the declarer respects your partner's defence, he might ask himself why West did not unblock in an attempt to avoid the throw-in, discarding his ace of spades and playing you for the king. But even good players miss this sort of inference occasionally. Of course, there are many declarers who would not under any circumstances jeopardize the safety of the contract for the sake of an overtrick, but experts make their own rules and tend to rely on their judgement in such situations.

The discarding of winners for deceptive purposes is a trick worth remembering. Most declarers will regard the inference that you cannot have an entry as infallible.

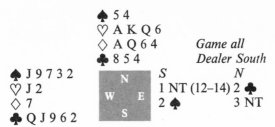

♠ 5 4
♡ A K Q 6
◇ A Q 6 4   *Game all*
♣ 8 5 4   *Dealer South*

♠ J 9 7 3 2
♡ J 2
◇ 7
♣ Q J 9 6 2

S	N
1 NT (12–14)	2 ♣
2 ♠	3 NT

When you lead the queen of clubs partner plays the ace and the declarer the ten. East returns the seven of clubs to the king, and South attacks diamonds, leading low to the ace and returning a low diamond to his king. East plays the knave on the second diamond and you throw the two of spades. Three rounds of hearts follow and you discard the three of spades. South then cashes the queen of diamonds. What do you discard?

Even if South's spades are no better than ace and queen he has two ways of making nine tricks, either by a direct spade finesse or by throwing you in with a club. Since you have nothing to lose, you may as well try to suggest a third line of play by discarding your knave of spades.

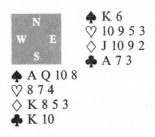

♠ K 6
♡ 10 9 5 3
◇ J 10 9 2
♣ A 7 3

♠ A Q 10 8
♡ 8 7 4
◇ K 8 5 3
♣ K 10

The discard of the knave of spades may lead South to fear that you started with six clubs and four spades headed by king and knave. If you started with six clubs, whether you had the king of spades or not, it would be safe for South to lead a spade to his ace at this point. If the king did not drop, he could still put East on lead and be sure of making another spade trick eventually.

♠ 10 7
♡ A 7   *Match-point pairs*
◇ A J 8 6 3   *N-S game*
♣ A J 6 5   *Dealer South*

♠ J 4
♡ Q 8 6 2
◇ 9 2
♣ K 10 9 7 3

S	N
1 ♠	2 ◇
2 ♠	3 ♣
3 NT	—

Your lead of the two of hearts draws the seven, nine and king, and South runs the queen of diamonds to your partner's king. East returns the four of hearts, and South enters hand with the ten of diamonds in order to lead the four of clubs. You put in the seven and East plays the two under dummy's knave. On the third and fourth diamonds you discard clubs while East and South each shed a spade. On the fifth diamond both East and South throw another spade. What about you?

Partner needs to have the ace of spades to defeat the contract, but South is more likely to have the ace and may have the queen as well. In that case a careless spade discard from you would allow South to make easy overtricks. To persuade South to hold himself to nine tricks you must discard the queen of hearts, which is what you would do if you held the king of spades.

♠ K 9 6 2
♡ J 10 9 4 3
◇ K 7 4
♣ 2

♠ A Q 8 5 3
♡ K 5
◇ Q 10 5
♣ Q 8 4

Note that the declarer will know the complete distribution when East discards a heart on the ace of clubs. If you have thrown a spade, he will know it is safe to take the finesse and score two overtricks. After all, you would hardly bare the king of spades when you had a safe alternative discard in the queen of hearts.

♠ A J 7 2
♡ Q 4
♢ K Q 8 4
♣ 8 6 3

Game all
Dealer South

♠ 10 3
♡ 10 9 8
♢ J 7 2
♣ Q 9 7 5 4

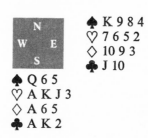

S	N
2 NT	3 ♣
3 ♡	3 ♠
3 NT	4 NT
6 NT	—

You lead the ten of hearts and dummy's queen wins. The declarer leads a second heart to his ace, and returns a spade to dummy's knave and your partner's king. East switches to the knave of clubs and South wins with the ace. The queen of spades is followed by a spade to the ace and you discard a club. South cashes the diamond king, leads a low diamond to his ace, East following with the three and nine, and then plays the king and knave of hearts. What do you discard on the fourth heart?

South must have the king of clubs, and since you know the diamonds are breaking, you can count his twelve tricks. Against an unimaginative declarer you have no chance, but an expert declarer will be worried about what to discard from dummy on the fourth heart. He has played his cards in the right order to bring off a double squeeze if you control the diamonds. You should try to persuade him that you have been squeezed in the minor suits by discarding the nine of clubs.

♠ K 9 8 4
♡ 7 6 5 2
♢ 10 9 3
♣ J 10

♠ Q 6 5
♡ A K J 3
♢ A 6 5
♣ A K 2

If South believes that you have been squeezed in clubs and diamonds, he will discard the small diamond from dummy on the fourth heart, relying on the lead of a diamond to the queen to squeeze East in the black suits. Bad luck!

No doubt you appreciated your partner's vital contribution to the defence. If he had not found that club switch, the declarer would have had an easy ride.

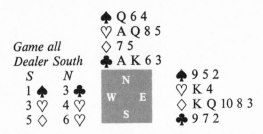

Game all
Dealer South

♠ Q 6 4
♡ A Q 8 5
♢ 7 5
♣ A K 6 3

♠ 9 5 2
♡ K 4
♢ K Q 10 8 3
♣ 9 7 2

S	N
1 ♠	3 ♣
3 ♡	4 ♡
5 ♢	6 ♡

West leads the queen of clubs to dummy's ace and, after ruffing a small club in hand, South runs the knave of hearts to your king. When you switch to the king of diamonds, South wins with the ace, leads a heart to the queen, discards a diamond on the king of clubs and ruffs the fourth club in hand. He then leads his last heart to the ace, West throwing the thirteenth club. What do you discard?

The declarer is likely to have the ace and king of spades, but can hardly have the knave or he would have laid down his hand. The critical case is where South's spades are headed by the ace, king and ten. Here you must try to persuade him to take a third-round finesse to your partner's knave by pretending to be squeezed in spades and diamonds. In other words, you should discard the ten and queen of diamonds on the third and fourth rounds of hearts, hanging on to three spades and the eight of diamonds. This risks nothing, for if South has the knave of diamonds and the queen does not appear, he will discard the knave and play for the drop in spades.

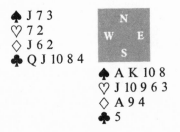

♠ J 7 3
♡ 7 2
♢ J 6 2
♣ Q J 10 8 4

♠ A K 10 8
♡ J 10 9 6 3
♢ A 9 4
♣ 5

♠ A Q 10 6 3
♡ A J
◇ A 4 2   *Love all*
♣ A 3 2   *Dealer North*

♠ J 9 5   *N   S*
♡ 9 8 7 3      1 ♠   1 NT
◇ K 5 3   3 NT —
♣ Q 9 4

On your lead of the nine of hearts the ace is played from dummy, East following with the five and South with the four. The two of clubs is led to South's knave and your queen, and after some thought you continue with a second heart. East wins with the king and switches to the ten of diamonds, which is allowed to hold the trick. On the nine of diamonds South again plays low and dummy's ace wins the trick. The declarer cashes the ace of clubs and leads a club to his king, East throwing a spade. When South cashes the queen and ten of hearts, East discards another spade. Then come two more rounds of clubs. What do you discard?

It seems that you did the wrong thing in leading a second heart instead of switching to a diamond, although South would probably have made the contract anyway. However, if South is a good card-reader, with a touch of greed in his make-up, you can still put him to the test by discarding one spade and the king of diamonds on the clubs. This will squeeze your partner, of course, and you must be able to rely on him to bare his king of spades without batting an eye. If South succumbs to the temptation to finesse the queen of spades for an overtrick, he will discover that he is not the only tricky player at the table.

          ♠ K 8 7 2
          ♡ K 6 5
          ◇ Q 10 9 8
          ♣ 7 6

♠ 4
♡ Q 10 4 2
◇ J 7 6
♣ K J 10 8 5

12 • The Third Opponent

The two defenders are generally supposed to be on the same side, but it is not uncommon, even in an expert game, to see them working at cross purposes. This would seem to suggest that in few partnerships is sufficient thought given to the art of defensive co-operation. In this chapter I propose to elaborate further upon the theme developed in *Killing Defence* under the heading 'To Love and to Cherish'.

We shall not concern ourselves too much with the standard defensive aids, such as conventional leads, trump and distributional echoes, and suit preference signals. These basic tools are invaluable, of course, and should be an integral part of every defender's equipment. Experienced players use them well, on the whole, and it is something more fundamental that lies at the root of most of their defensive disasters. It is a failure of imagination that leads to a break-down in logic somewhere along the line.

Many of the most expensive errors occur in situations where the defenders have to cash their tricks in a hurry because the declarer will make his contract as soon as he regains the lead. When a defender goes astray in a cash-out situation it is normally for one of two reasons. Either he has misinterpreted the information supplied by his partner, or his partner has fed him the wrong information.

As a partnership exercise, defenders need to spend some time discussing the simple logic of such situations to make sure that they are operating on the same wavelength. It is important to agree not only on the conclusions to be drawn from a particular action but also on the negative inferences that are available when the action is not taken.

But how can you be sure of passing the correct data across the table? This is where imagination has a part to play. You must acquire the knack of putting yourself in your partner's place and considering what his problem will be when he gains the lead. Once you appreciate his problem you are half way towards finding a means of telling him the answer. If your hand contains an unexpected feature—an improbable void, for instance—consider how you can best indicate the fact to partner. There will usually be a logical way if only you can think of it. Train yourself to regard it as your mistake when partner goes wrong through lack of information.

One principle of defence is absolutely basic. As soon as a player sees a way to defeat the contract he should take charge to make sure the defence is conducted on the proper lines. Much recrimination is caused by the frequent neglect of this principle. A defender sees how to defeat the contract but still waits for his partner to make the first move. Partner gives his well-known imitation of a stuffed marrow and the contract is made. The disaster may not be entirely due to lack of initiative. Sometimes a player feels that his partner will regard it as an insult if matters are taken out of his hands. Personally, I am happy to be insulted in this manner.

Players tend to forget that what is plain to them may be far from plain to a partner who does not have all the relevant data. It is right to take charge when there is the slightest risk that partner will misdefend. That means always.

The corollary is, of course, that when you are unsure about the correct line of defence you should not hazard a guess but leave matters to your partner, who may be better informed. Never take charge without good reason. Respect your partner's judgement when he favours a particular line of defence, and he will do the same for you. Intelligent co-operation based on mutual confidence will enable you to keep guesswork to a minimum.

Here is a typical partnership problem.

♠ K Q 8
♡ 10 8 3
◇ A K Q 10
♣ J 10 7

Love all
Dealer North

N	S
1 ◇	1 ♡
1 NT	4 ♡

♠ A 7 6
♡ 6 2
◇ 8 7 5 3
♣ A Q 5 2

The lead of the knave of spades is covered by dummy's king. You win with the ace and return the seven of spades, and partner's nine forces out the queen. When the eight of hearts is run, West wins with the king and switches to the king of clubs. How should you defend?

It looks like a cash-out situation, because South has probably six trumps. Five trump tricks, one spade and four diamonds will see him home. What does partner mean by this odd lead of the king of clubs? The answer is waiting if you apply your mind to the problem. Although realizing that you need to have the ace of clubs to defeat the contract, partner wishes to retain the lead in his hand. This can only mean that he has five spades and is wondering whether he can cash the ten or not. West expects you to play low if you have no more spades, and to encourage a club continuation if you have a third spade.

The five of clubs might be encouraging enough, but it would be foolish to take the chance. If West is in doubt there can be no spade to cash. It is therefore your duty to play the ace on partner's king and continue with the queen of clubs.

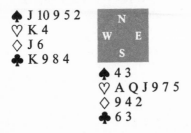

♠ J 10 9 5 2
♡ K 4
◇ J 6
♣ K 9 8 4

♠ 4 3
♡ A Q J 9 7 5
◇ 9 4 2
♣ 6 3

Game all
Dealer South

S	N
2 ♠	2 NT
4 ♠	—

♠ —
♡ 9 6 5 2
◇ J 10 7 6 5
♣ K Q 7 3

♠ 7 4
♡ K 8 3
◇ K 9 8 2
♣ A J 6 5

West leads the queen of hearts, you encourage with the eight, and South wins with the ace. On the ace, king and knave of spades partner follows with the three, ten and queen while you discard the two of diamonds. West continues with the knave of hearts. How do you defend?

The declarer has seven spade tricks, the ace of hearts and presumably the ace of diamonds for his bidding. If he has the queen of diamonds as well, there is some danger of your being thrown in eventually with the ace of clubs. If South started with only two hearts it could be right to overtake the knave of hearts with your king, cash the ace of clubs and exit with your third heart. But this plan would be fatal if South started with three hearts and a void in clubs.

You cannot tell what to do and should not, therefore, try to master-mind the situation. Play the three of hearts and leave the decision to West. Holding three hearts, partner will continue with a third round, after which you can safely play the ace of clubs. With four hearts, West will know there are no more to cash and will switch to a club to protect your exit card.

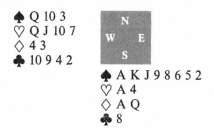

♣ Q 10 3
♡ Q J 10 7
◇ 4 3
♣ 10 9 4 2

♠ A K J 9 8 6 5 2
♡ A 4
◇ A Q
♣ 8

When you need help from partner it is advisable to give him every chance to provide it.

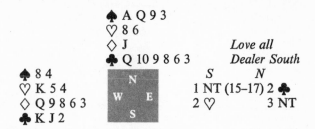

```
                    ♠ A Q 9 3
                    ♡ 8 6
                    ◇ J                    Love all
                    ♣ Q 10 9 8 6 3        Dealer South
        ♠ 8 4                      S      N
        ♡ K 5 4                   1 NT (15–17) 2 ♣
        ◇ Q 9 8 6 3              2 ♡         3 NT
        ♣ K J 2
```

On your lead of the six of diamonds partner produces the king. The declarer wins with the ace and plays the ace and another club. How do you defend?

Since South cannot come to nine tricks without developing the club suit, there is no hurry for you to win the trick. You should play the knave of clubs on the second round in order to make sure of seeing at least one discard from partner.

```
                    ♠ 10 7 6 2
                    ♡ A 10 7 3
                    ◇ K 7 4
                    ♣ 5 4

        ♠ K J 5
        ♡ Q J 9 2
        ◇ A 10 5 2
        ♣ A 7
```

With the layout as above, partner's ten of hearts on the third round of clubs will leave you in no doubt as to how to continue, and the contract will be defeated by three tricks. If you had gone up with the king of clubs on the second round you would have been faced with a blind guess and the odds would have been against your getting it right.

When the declarer has to develop a suit, the general rule is to hold off for as long as possible. Not only does this permit the exchange of the maximum information, but it also helps partner to count the declarer's hand.

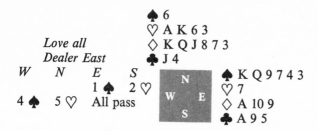

♠ 6
♡ A K 6 3
◊ K Q J 8 7 3
♣ J 4

Love all
Dealer East

W	N	E	S
		1 ♠	2 ♡
4 ♠	5 ♡	All pass	

♠ K Q 9 7 4 3
♡ 7
◊ A 10 9
♣ A 9 5

West leads the two of diamonds and you capture dummy's king with your ace. How should you continue?

The two of diamonds is an obvious singleton, which opens up the possibility of defeating the contract by two tricks. All you have to do is give partner a ruff, regain the lead with the ace of clubs, and give partner a second ruff for two down.

Unfortunately, your nine of diamonds is too high a card to convey a clear message about your preference for a club return. West is all too likely to return a spade, the suit you bid, and if the declarer has the ace he will be able to make his contract by drawing trumps and discarding his losing clubs on dummy's diamonds.

It does not pay to be too greedy. To avoid any chance of a misunderstanding you should cash the ace of clubs before giving partner his diamond ruff.

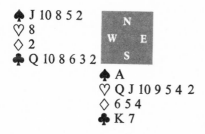

♠ J 10 8 5 2
♡ 8
◊ 2
♣ Q 10 8 6 3 2

♠ A
♡ Q J 10 9 5 4 2
◊ 6 5 4
♣ K 7

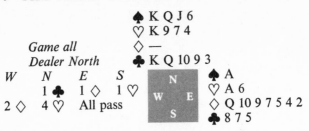

Game all
Dealer North

♠ K Q J 6
♡ K 9 7 4
◇ —
♣ K Q 10 9 3

W	N	E	S
	1 ♣	1 ◇	1 ♡
2 ◇	4 ♡	All pass	

♠ A
♡ A 6
◇ Q 10 9 7 5 4 2
♣ 8 7 5

When West leads the ten of spades, the king is played from the table and your ace wins the trick. How should you continue?

To defeat this contract you must somehow put partner on lead to give you a spade ruff. There appears to be no hope unless West has the ace of clubs. The difficulty is that partner has no reason to suspect that you can ruff the second round of spades. If you lead a club to partner's ace at this stage he is very likely to return the suit, thinking it is a club ruff you are angling for.

Since you have trump control, there is no need to rush matters To give partner a chance of coming to the right conclusion you should first play a diamond. When the declarer wins either in his hand or in dummy and leads a trump, you plan to step in immediately with the ace and switch to the eight of clubs. Partner will realize that this is not a singleton since you did not return it at the first opportunity. On winning with the ace, he will reason that the only remaining chance is to switch back to spades.

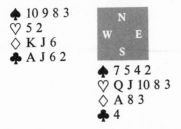

♠ 10 9 8 3
♡ 5 2
◇ K J 6
♣ A J 6 2

♠ 7 5 4 2
♡ Q J 10 8 3
◇ A 8 3
♣ 4

♠ 9 8 5 2
♡ 10 6
◇ Q 5 4   *N-S game*
♣ K J 7 3   *Dealer South*

♠ A K 10 7   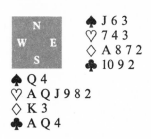   S   W   N   E
♡ K 5   1 ♡   1 ♠   —   —
◇ J 10 9 6   3 ♡   —   4 ♡   All pass
♣ 8 6 5

On your lead of the ace of spades partner plays the three and declarer the four. You switch to the knave of diamonds, which draws a low card from dummy, the eight from partner and the king from declarer. Entering dummy with the lead of a low club to the knave, South runs the ten of hearts to your king. How should you continue?

It appears that partner has the ace of diamonds, but it would be a grave dereliction of duty for you to lead a second diamond at this point. The declarer would put up the queen from the table and East, on winning with the ace, would be operating in the dark. He is not to know that you made an off-beat overcall in a four-card suit and he would probably try to take the setting trick in diamonds, which could be fatal if the declarer began with only two diamonds.

You must therefore cash the king of spades before leading a second diamond. You can be confident that the king of spades will stand up, for with four spades to the queen and knave, as well as the ace of diamonds, partner would surely have raised your overcall.

                              ♠ J 6 3
                              ♡ 7 4 3
                              ◇ A 8 7 2
                              ♣ 10 9 2
            ♠ Q 4
            ♡ A Q J 9 8 2
            ◇ K 3
            ♣ A Q 4

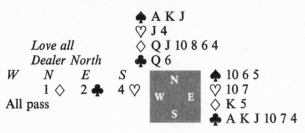

Love all
Dealer North

W	N	E	S
	1 ◇	2 ♣	4 ♡
All pass			

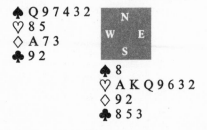

♠ A K J
♡ J 4
◇ Q J 10 8 6 4
♣ Q 6

♠ 10 6 5
♡ 10 7
◇ K 5
♣ A K J 10 7 4

West leads the nine of clubs, you capture the queen with your king, and South plays the three. When you continue with the ace of clubs, the declarer plays the five and your partner the two. What now?

If partner has queen and another trump, a third round of clubs will promote a trump trick for him, after which he may be able to take the setting trick with the ace of diamonds. The alternative is to try for two tricks in diamonds. Which line of defence do you choose?

In fact, there is no need to commit yourself, for you can enlist partner's help by means of an asking play. The proper course, since you always need at least one diamond trick, is to lead the king of diamonds and see what reaction it produces. If partner plays an encouraging card you can continue with a second diamond. If he discourages, it will mean that he has a promotable trump.

♠ Q 9 7 4 3 2
♡ 8 5
◇ A 7 3
♣ 9 2

♠ 8
♡ A K Q 9 6 3 2
◇ 9 2
♣ 8 5 3

No matter which card the declarer plays under the king of diamonds your partner's seven tells you to continue the suit.

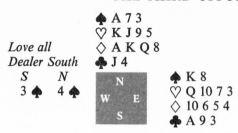

♠ A 7 3
♡ K J 9 5
◇ A K Q 8
♣ J 4

Love all
Dealer South

S   N
3 ♠   4 ♠

♠ K 8
♡ Q 10 7 3
◇ 10 6 5 4
♣ A 9 3

West leads the five of clubs and South plays the seven under your ace. How should you continue?

In view of the strong dummy it is not hard to see that the contract can be defeated only if your partner has the king of clubs and the ace of hearts. But can you see the risk involved in returning a club at this point?

Look at it from your partner's point of view, when he wins the second trick with the king of clubs. To West it will appear highly improbable that you have a trump trick on the bidding, and he may well decide that the best chance is to try for two heart tricks by underleading his ace. And that, of course, would enable the declarer to make crowing noises and his contract.

On this hand it is up to you to save partner from an excess of imagination. You can keep him straight quite simply by returning the three of hearts at the second trick. He will then have no option but to take his ace and cash the king of clubs, and the contract will be defeated when the spade finesse fails.

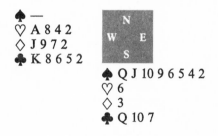

♠ —
♡ A 8 4 2
◇ J 9 7 2
♣ K 8 6 5 2

♠ Q J 10 9 6 5 4 2
♡ 6
◇ 3
♣ Q 10 7

♠ K J 5
♡ K Q 8 4
◇ K J 6 4   *Game all*
♣ A K   *Dealer North*

♠ 9 8 3   N   S
♡ 2   2 NT   3 ♡
◇ A 10 9 5   4 ♣   4 ♡
♣ J 9 6 5 3

On your lead of the nine of spades the five is played from the table and partner's ace wins the trick. East returns the eight of diamonds on which South plays the two. How do you defend?

For the contract to be defeated, partner will need to have the ace of trumps and will also need to score a diamond ruff. If he has a singleton diamond you ought to win at once and return the suit, but if he has a doubleton you must duck on the first round in order to preserve your entry. Is there any clue to the correct play?

With a reliable partner, who is well trained in the language of defence, this is not a matter of guesswork. There is a clear indication that East will have a doubleton diamond. With a singleton, he would first have cashed the ace of trumps so that you would have had no option but to win the first round of diamonds.

You should, therefore, play the nine of diamonds at trick two. East will win the first round of trumps, lead his second diamond and ruff your diamond return to put the contract one down.

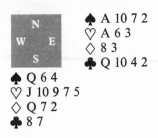

♠ A 10 7 2
♡ A 6 3
◇ 8 3
♣ Q 10 4 2

♠ Q 6 4
♡ J 10 9 7 5
◇ Q 7 2
♣ 8 7

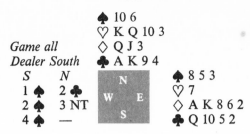

```
                    ♠ 10 6
                    ♡ K Q 10 3
   Game all         ◇ Q J 3
   Dealer South     ♣ A K 9 4
     S     N                      ♠ 8 5 3
     1 ♠   2 ♣                    ♡ 7
     2 ♠   3 NT                   ◇ A K 8 6 2
     4 ♠   —                      ♣ Q 10 5 2
```

West leads the ten of diamonds and the knave is played from the table. How do you plan the defence?

Even if partner has a doubleton diamond, he will also need the ace of hearts or a trump trick if the contract is to be defeated. And if he has the ace of hearts or a trump trick, he does not need the diamond ruff, for you can negotiate a heart ruff instead.

If you win with the king of diamonds and lead the heart, however, your intentions will not be clear. Partner may win and switch back to the nine of diamonds, hoping to give you three tricks in the suit. It might therefore seem a good idea to win the first trick with the ace of diamonds and switch to the heart. Partner would certainly not return a diamond then, but he might duck the ace of hearts, playing you for a doubleton heart and the ace of trumps.

Since you need two diamond tricks in any case, the proper course is to take the king of diamonds and cash the ace before switching to the heart. If partner has the ace, he will then have no reason to duck.

```
   ♠ 7 2
   ♡ A 9 8 4
   ◇ 10 9 5
   ♣ J 8 7 3
                    ♠ A K Q J 9 4
                    ♡ J 6 5 2
                    ◇ 7 4
                    ♣ 6
```

South would have been better advised to have passed three no trumps.

Game all
Dealer South

♠ A J 10 5
♥ K 8 7 6 3
♦ 7
♣ 9 6 3

♠ K 6 3
♥ 4
♦ 9 8 5 4 2
♣ Q J 5 4

S	N
1 ♥	4 ♥

West leads the king of clubs, which, according to your partnership agreement, cannot be from ace, king and others. How do you defend?

It seems unlikely that West would lead an unsupported king on this bidding, so he probably has the doubleton ace and king. In that case, there is a chance of scoring three club tricks and the king of spades, although the declarer may be able to discard dummy's third club before you gain the lead. At all events you must make it plain tô partner that you want a spade switch, not a diamond, after the second club.

To play the queen of clubs on the first round will not do. Partner would take that as showing solid clubs, and when you followed with the five on the next round he might switch to diamonds with disastrous results. You must do it the other way round, playing the five on the first club and the queen on the second. This will be an unmistakable suit preference signal for a spade switch.

♠ Q 7 4
♥ 10 9 5
♦ Q J 10 6 3
♣ A K

♠ 9 8 2
♥ A Q J 2
♦ A K
♣ 10 8 7 2

On the spade switch, South can get rid of dummy's club loser only by going up with the ace, which establishes two spade tricks for the defence.

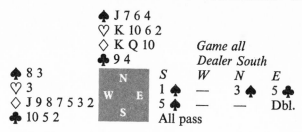

```
                    ♠ J 7 6 4
                    ♡ K 10 6 2
                    ◇ K Q 10          Game all
                    ♣ 9 4             Dealer South
♠ 8 3                          S      W     N     E
♡ 3                            1 ♠    —     3 ♠   5 ♣
◇ J 9 8 7 5 3 2                5 ♠    —     —     Dbl.
♣ 10 5 2                       All pass
```

Your lead of the singleton heart works out well when partner produces the ace, declarer playing the four, East returns the knave of hearts and South plays the five. You ruff and dutifully lead the nine of diamonds to dummy's king and partner's ace. East leads the nine of hearts on which South plays the queen and you ruff again. What do you lead now?

On the face of it the nine of hearts looks like a further suit preference signal requesting another diamond return, but if you examine this notion more closely it does not stand up. Holding the singleton ace of diamonds and a trump to ruff with, partner would surely have cashed the ace at the second trick, before returning the knave of hearts.

The logical explanation is that the nine of hearts is your partner's last card in the suit, in which case no suit preference indication can be obtained from it. The time has come to lead a club in order to make sure of exacting the full penalty.

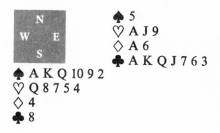

```
                              ♠ 5
                              ♡ A J 9
                              ◇ A 6
                              ♣ A K Q J 7 6 3
          ♠ A K Q 10 9 2
          ♡ Q 8 7 5 4
          ◇ 4
          ♣ 8
```

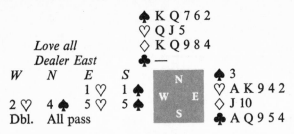

♠ K Q 7 6 2
♡ Q J 5
Love all   ◇ K Q 9 8 4
Dealer East   ♣ —

W	N	E	S
	1 ♡	1 ♠	
2 ♡	4 ♣	5 ♡	5 ♠
Dbl.	All pass		

♠ 3
♡ A K 9 4 2
◇ J 10
♣ A Q 9 5 4

West leads the six of hearts upon which dummy plays the five, you the king and South the ten. How should you continue?

For his double, partner should have either the ace of trumps or the ace of diamonds, but he can hardly have both. That means you will need two heart tricks to defeat the contract, and you can be confident of scoring them in spite of South's play of the ten. Partner would hardly have led the six from 8 7 6 3, so the declarer must be concealing a second heart.

Don't make the mistake of switching to the knave of diamonds at this point. That would lead partner to assume that no more hearts could be cashed. If he has the ace of diamonds there is nothing more certain than that he would return a diamond in the hope of giving you a ruff.

It is up to you to make the position clear by cashing your second heart before leading the knave of diamonds.

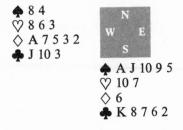

♠ 8 4
♡ 8 6 3
◇ A 7 5 3 2
♣ J 10 3

♠ A J 10 9 5
♡ 10 7
◇ 6
♣ K 8 7 6 2

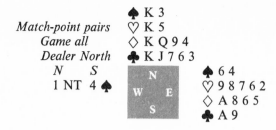

♠ K 3
♡ K 5
◇ K Q 9 4
♣ K J 7 6 3

Match-point pairs
Game all
Dealer North

N   S
1 NT 4 ♠

♠ 6 4
♡ 9 8 7 6 2
◇ A 8 6 5
♣ A 9

West leads the two of clubs and you capture dummy's knave with your ace. Your trump return goes to dummy's king and the declarer draws two more rounds with the ace and queen, West following with the seven, nine and knave while dummy throws a club, and you, a heart. The declarer then leads the three of diamonds upon which West plays the ten and dummy the king. How do you defend?

Partner's ten must indicate a doubleton diamond, which gives the declarer six spades, three diamonds and a club, for a total of ten tricks. The contract cannot be defeated and your ambition must be limited to scoring a third trick for the defence. The third trick can only be the ace of hearts, but it would be a big mistake to win your ace of diamonds and lead a heart. Having no means of knowing that the declarer has three diamond tricks, partner might well allow the king of hearts to win, hoping to score two tricks in the suit. And that would give the declarer an easy overtrick.

You have several ways of putting partner in the picture, the simplest of which is to hold up the ace of diamonds.

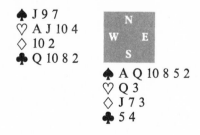

♠ J 9 7
♡ A J 10 4
◇ 10 2
♣ Q 10 8 2

♠ A Q 10 8 5 2
♡ Q 3
◇ J 7 3
♣ 5 4

13 • Improvising

First-class dummy players are reasonably thick on the ground, but the really good defender is a rare bird indeed. This seems a little surprising when one considers that we play two hands in defence for every one we play as declarer. Clearly, practice does not necessarily make for perfection. The explanation lies partly in the attitude of mind. Many players regard defending as a disagreeable chore that has to be performed while waiting for the next moment of real living when they have a chance to play another hand.

The preference for playing the dummy is easy to understand, for the declarer has by far the simpler task. From the moment that dummy goes down the declarer can see what his problems are and set about solving them. Routine situations are well documented, and in many cases all the declarer has to do is raid his memory banks for the appropriate technique to deal with the hand.

Defence is difficult, because problems are more obscure and technique less well defined. Groping in the dark, the defender frequently finds himself required to improvise a weapon to fit the occasion. This calls for a flexible mind and ability to look beyond the obvious course of action.

The truly expert defender accepts no limitations to his freedom of action. He is a pragmatist with scant respect for slogans and rules of thumb, prepared to reject standard practice and violate all the accepted maxims of defence when his judgement tells him that the moment is right to do so. It is his supreme confidence in his own judgement that makes him such an unpredictable and formidable adversary.

You will need to think like an expert to solve the problems in this final chapter.

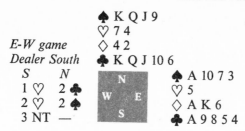

E-W game
Dealer South

♠ K Q J 9
♡ 7 4
◇ 4 2
♣ K Q J 10 6

♠ A 10 7 3
♡ 5
◇ A K 6
♣ A 9 8 5 4

S	N
1 ♡	2 ♣
2 ♡	2 ♠
3 NT	—

West leads the three of diamonds against the impertinent three no trump contract. How do you defend?

Holding four top tricks in your own hand, you cannot rely on partner for much. His diamonds are likely to be headed by the knave rather than the queen. One idea that springs to mind is to win the first trick with the ace and return the six of diamonds, hoping to steal a trick for partner's knave. But the declarer should not go wrong, for with ace, knave and six the knave would be your proper return.

South's show of strength by his third-round jump to three no trumps must surely indicate a solid six-card heart suit. In that case he can have only three cards in the black suits and it must be possible to cut him off from dummy. You cannot be sure of doing the right thing, but South's doubleton is more likely to be in spades than in clubs. After winning the first trick, therefore, you should lead a small spade.

♠ 8 6 4
♡ 10 8 3 2
◇ J 9 7 3
♣ 7 2

♠ 5 2
♡ A K Q J 9 6
◇ Q 10 8 5
♣ 3

South can cash no more than seven tricks before giving you the lead again. When he does, you will cash all your tops and exit with the six of diamonds and partner will eventually score the setting trick.

♠ A J 3
♡ K Q 7 5
◇ 9 3   *N-S game*
♣ Q J 9 4   *Dealer South*

♠ K 10 9
♡ A 2
◇ Q J 10 7 4
♣ K 8 3

S	W	N	E
1 ♡	Dbl.	Rdbl.	—
—	2 ◇	4 ♡	All pass

On your lead of the diamond queen East plays the two. South wins with the ace and leads the six of hearts. How do you defend?

Since partner cannot help in diamonds, you will need three tricks from the black suits. South is marked with the ace of clubs, but it is just possible for East to have the queen of spades. The text-books tell you to lead the ten to trap dummy's knave, but that may not be good enough in this case. South would cover with the knave and win the spade return with the ace. After drawing trumps and eliminating diamonds, he would throw you in with the third spade to make what could be a fatal return,

Unorthodox play is needed to ensure that partner wins his spade trick at the right moment. After winning the first round of trumps you must lead the king of spades.

♠ Q 6 5
♡ 4 3
◇ 8 6 5 2
♣ 10 7 6 2

♠ 8 7 4 2
♡ J 10 9 8 6
◇ A K
♣ A 5

Note that it would be dangerous to duck the first trump. The declarer might switch to ace and another club and eventually discard two losing spades on the third and fourth clubs.

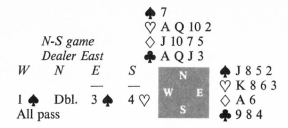

♠ 7
♥ A Q 10 2
N-S game   ◇ J 10 7 5
Dealer East ♣ A Q J 3

W	N	E	S
—	—		
1 ♠	Dbl.	3 ♠	4 ♥
All pass			

♠ J 8 5 2
♥ K 8 6 3
◇ A 6
♣ 9 8 4

After having a look with the ace of spades, West switches to the eight of diamonds. South plays the three under your ace and wins the diamond continuation with the king, West playing the two and dummy the knave. The four of hearts is led to the knave, queen and three. After a moment's thought the declarer continues with the ten of hearts from the table. You take the king this time and partner discards the five of clubs. What now?

From the play of the diamonds it seems certain that partner began with a doubleton and the declarer with five. If South has two clubs as well, he will come to ten tricks by finessing twice in clubs. The defence has a chance only if South has three spades and a singleton club. Even then, a spade lead from you will be fatal, for South will ruff with dummy's ace, draw trumps, finessing against your eight, and score ten tricks with the aid of the club finesse.

A trump return looks safer, and will certainly prevent the spade ruff, but if South has the queen of spades, the play of two more rounds of trumps, followed by three rounds of diamonds, will squeeze partner in the black suits. The only way to break up the squeeze is to return a club.

♠ A K 9 6 3
♥ J
◇ 8 2
♣ K 10 7 5 2

♠ Q 10 4
♥ 9 7 5 4
◇ K Q 9 4 3
♣ 6

```
              ♠ J 7 3
              ♡ 9 7 6
              ◇ J 10 5        Game all
              ♣ K Q 10 5      Dealer South
♠ Q 10 8        N        S      W      N      E
♡ K Q                    1 ♡    Dbl.   1 NT   —
◇ A K 6 2    W     E     4 ♡    All pass
♣ A 9 7 3       S
```

When you lead the ace of diamonds, partner plays the eight and declarer the three. You continue with the king and another diamond, but all follow and the declarer wins the third round with the queen. South plays ace and another heart, East following suit with the two and five, and you are on lead again. What now?

Presumably no defender will be rash enough to lead the thirteenth diamond. The sanguine will attempt to cash the ace of clubs, while the more sophisticated will try a lead of the ten of spades. But all these moves are fraught with danger. There is a completely safe defence that will always defeat the contract, although only the experts are likely to consider such an improbable play. It is the lead of a small club.

Once it occurs to you, this lead stands out. South is marked with three diamonds and not more than six trumps. He must therefore have four cards in the black suits. Even if he has a singleton club, the lead of a low club can never present him with the contract. Eventually, he will have to concede either a spade or a club trick to the defence.

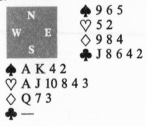

```
           N        ♠ 9 6 5
                    ♡ 5 2
       W      E     ◇ 9 8 4
           S        ♣ J 8 6 4 2
      ♠ A K 4 2
      ♡ A J 10 8 4 3
      ◇ Q 7 3
      ♣ —
```

♠ Q 6
♡ 8 7 2
Love all   ◇ A K Q 10 5
Dealer South   ♣ J 9 4

S	N
1 ♠	2 ◇
2 ♠	3 ♠
4 ♠	—

♠ A 8
♡ A 4
◇ J 9 6 2
♣ K 10 6 5 3

West leads the queen of hearts and South plays the three under your ace. How should you continue?

It seems reasonable to hope for three tricks in hearts and clubs in addition to your trump ace. The trouble is that you may not have time to establish them. South is likely to have six good trumps and the ace of clubs, as well as the king of hearts. Whether you return a heart or a club, he will win, knock out the ace of trumps, regain the lead before you can cash enough tricks, draw trumps, and make ten tricks with the aid of the diamond suit.

However, if the declarer has three losers in hearts and clubs he can have no more than two diamonds. In that case an effective defence may be possible, if you get your priorities right. You must abandon a heart or club attack for the meantime and switch to a diamond. You will subsequently hold up your ace of trumps until the second round and lead another diamond, cutting the last link with dummy. Partner's remaining trump will prevent the declarer from enjoying a third diamond, and you will eventually score those tricks that are due to you in the other suits.

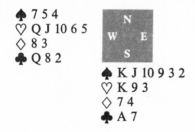

♠ 7 5 4
♡ Q J 10 6 5
◇ 8 3
♣ Q 8 2

♠ K J 10 9 3 2
♡ K 9 3
◇ 7 4
♣ A 7

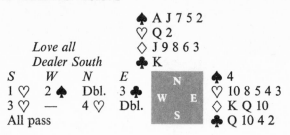

```
                        ♠ A J 7 5 2
                        ♡ Q 2
        Love all        ◇ J 9 8 6 3
        Dealer South    ♣ K
     S    W    N    E              ♠ 4
     1♡   2♠   Dbl.  3♣            ♡ 10 8 5 4 3
     3♡   —    4♡   Dbl.          ◇ K Q 10
     All pass                      ♣ Q 10 4 2
```

Partner's jump overcall shows five cards in each of the black suits and a hand of limited strength. West leads the king of spades and the ace wins the trick. When the king of clubs is played from the table, partner wins with the ace and continues with the queen of spades. How do you plan the defence?

A count of the declarer's tricks will save you from going wrong here. South can have no side winners, apart from the aces of spades and diamonds, and you will defeat the contract for certain if you can prevent him from making eight tricks from his trumps. If South has six trumps, however, your partner will have no trump to lead. It is up to you to prevent two club ruffs in dummy by ruffing your partner's winning spade and returning a trump.

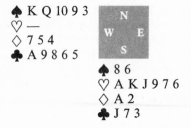

```
     ♠ K Q 10 9 3
     ♡ —
     ◇ 7 5 4
     ♣ A 9 8 6 5

                        ♠ 8 6
                        ♡ A K J 9 7 6
                        ◇ A 2
                        ♣ J 7 3
```

If you had allowed West to hold the trick with the queen of spades, there would have been no further opportunity to defeat the contract.

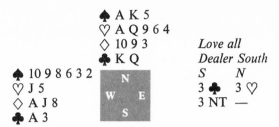

♠ A K 5
♡ A Q 9 6 4
◇ 10 9 3   *Love all*
♣ K Q   *Dealer South*

♠ 10 9 8 6 3 2   S   N
♡ J 5   3 ♣   3 ♡
◇ A J 8   3 NT   —
♣ A 3

On your lead of the ten of spades dummy plays the five and East the knave. South wins with the queen and leads the two of clubs. How do you plan the defence?

Partner will need to have good hearts if this contract is to be defeated, for on the bidding, South is marked with something in diamonds. Clearly you must take your ace of clubs on the first round so as to block the suit, but the obvious spade continuation, or even a heart switch, may not be good enough. If the declarer has both king and queen of diamonds it will be vital to knock out his entry before clubs can be unblocked.

There is only one sure way of knocking out the diamond entry and that is by making the unorthodox return of the knave of diamonds at trick three.

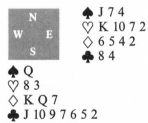

♠ J 7 4
♡ K 10 7 2
◇ 6 5 4 2
♣ 8 4

♠ Q
♡ 8 3
◇ K Q 7
♣ J 10 9 7 6 5 2

After your return of the knave of diamonds, the declarer has to abandon all hope of bringing in the club suit. No doubt he will turn to hearts instead, but careful defence will defeat the contract.

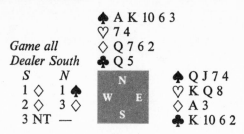

♠ A K 10 6 3
♡ 7 4
◇ Q 7 6 2
♣ Q 5

Game all
Dealer South

S	N
1 ◇	1 ♠
2 ◇	3 ◇
3 NT	—

♠ Q J 7 4
♡ K Q 8
◇ A 3
♣ K 10 6 2

West leads the five of hearts and the declarer plays the two under your queen. How should you continue?

On the bidding, partner can hardly have the ace of hearts, although he may have the knave. Even so, there can be no future in establishing the heart suit, for West cannot have an outside entry. South would simply win the third round, knock out your ace of diamonds, and make nine tricks in one way or another.

Is there anything else worth trying? Well, if partner has the knave of clubs, a club lead from his side of the table might establish three club tricks for the defence. And a player of imagination should not find it too difficult to put West on lead. Just return the eight of hearts at trick two.

♠ 9 8 2
♡ J 9 6 5 3
◇ 9
♣ J 8 7 4

♠ 5
♡ A 10 2
◇ K J 10 8 5 4
♣ A 9 3

The declarer is sure to duck the second heart, for he has no means of knowing that your partner's lead was not from K J 9 5 3. On winning a surprise trick with the knave of hearts, partner ought to be able to work out what is required of him.

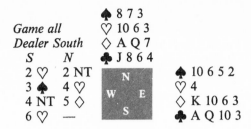

```
              ♠ 8 7 3
Game all      ♡ 10 6 3
Dealer South  ◇ A Q 7
  S    N      ♣ J 8 6 4
  2 ♡  2 NT        ♠ 10 6 5 2
  3 ♠  4 ♡         ♡ 4
  4 NT 5 ◇         ◇ K 10 6 3
  6 ♡   —          ♣ A Q 10 3
```

West leads the two of clubs and South plays the seven under your ace. How do you continue?

Although South cannot conceivably have a second club loser, it seems natural to return the suit and let him get on with things. But it is worth while giving a little thought to the bidding. To account for his use of Blackwood, South's shape must surely be 5-6-1-1. If partner has a trump trick, you have nothing to worry about, but if not, the setting trick will have to come from spades. That means partner's singleton will need to be an honour card, and the declarer will have to be cut off from the table before he discovers that a third-round spade finesse is required.

Now the correct line of defence is becoming clear. You must return a diamond into the jaws of dummy's tenace.

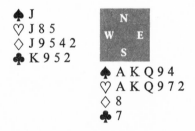

```
♠ J
♡ J 8 5
◇ J 9 5 4 2
♣ K 9 5 2
              ♠ A K Q 9 4
              ♡ A K Q 9 7 2
              ◇ 8
              ♣ 7
```

The unorthodox return gives the declarer an extra diamond trick which does him no good at all, for he is unable to avoid an eventual spade loser.

```
                    ♠ K
                    ♡ K J 4
                    ◇ K Q 9 8 6 3    Love all
                    ♣ K 8 3          Dealer East
     ♠ 9 2                 W    N    E         S
     ♡ Q 7 3                              1 NT (12–14) 2 ♠
     ◇ 10 4                3 ♣  3 NT  —         4 ♠
     ♣ A 10 9 7 6 2        All pass
```

You lead the ten of diamonds and dummy's king wins the trick. After cashing the king of spades, South plays the three of diamonds from the table and East wins with the knave. East switches to the queen of clubs, South plays the five and you take the ace. How should you continue?

Presumably partner refused to lead the ace of diamonds for fear that South would discard a singleton club instead of ruffing. East is marked with the ace of hearts, however, so you can put him back on lead to send the diamond through. That will force South to ruff high, and if East's trumps are as good as J 10 x or 10 x x x they will score the setting trick.

Have we overlooked any snags? Well, if partner has 10 x x x in trumps, the declarer might, if he reads the position correctly, shorten his trumps and bring off a coup, using the knave and king of hearts as entries to dummy. To prevent that happening you must lead, not a small heart, but the queen.

```
              N         ♠ 10 7 5 4
          W       E     ♡ A 8 6
              S         ◇ A J 5
                        ♣ Q J 4
     ♠ A Q J 8 6 3
     ♡ 10 9 5 2
     ◇ 7 2
     ♣ 5
```

Double-dummy, the declarer can always make his contract if he leaves the king of spades on the table and leads another diamond at trick two.

```
                    ♠ 9 5
                    ♡ 9 8 4 3
   Game all         ◇ A Q 10
   Dealer South     ♣ K Q 7 5
      S     N                    ♠ J 3
      1 ♠   2 ♣                  ♡ K Q J 7
      3 ♠   4 ♠                  ◇ K J 5 3
                                 ♣ 9 8 6
```

West leads the nine of diamonds, the queen is played from the table, and South plays the four under your king. How should you continue?

Prospects are not very bright since the declarer has advertised seven playing tricks. If South has a trump loser, he will certainly have the aces of both hearts and clubs, which gives the defence no chance. But South might have six top trumps and only one of the outside aces, presumably the ace of hearts, since he did not put up the ace of diamonds and claim ten tricks.

A heart attack is indicated and the defence will have no chance unless South has three cards in the suit. What about the club position? On the bidding, South is not likely to be void in clubs. He might have a singleton club and three cards in each of the red suits, but in that case a switch to the king of hearts will not be good enough. South will hold off once, win the second heart and lead his club, which West will have to duck. After running all his trumps, South would then throw you in to lead up to the diamond tenace.

If South has two clubs and two diamonds, a switch to the king of hearts fares no better. South will duck, win the second round, lead a club to the queen, draw trumps and lead another club, eventually discarding his second heart loser.

To defeat this contract you must put yourself in a position to attack the ace of diamonds, if the declarer ducks a heart. It cannot be done from your side of the table. The threat to the ace of diamonds must come from your partner, and that will be possible only if he has the ten of hearts. You should therefore switch to the seven of hearts at trick two. This play may give away an overtrick, but that is a small price to pay for a chance of beating the contract.

The full hand:

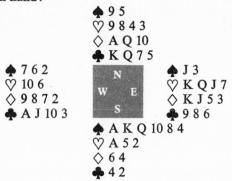

```
                  ♠ 9 5
                  ♡ 9 8 4 3
                  ◇ A Q 10
                  ♣ K Q 7 5
   ♠ 7 6 2                      ♠ J 3
   ♡ 10 6                       ♡ K Q J 7
   ◇ 9 8 7 2                    ◇ K J 5 3
   ♣ A J 10 3                   ♣ 9 8 6
                  ♠ A K Q 10 8 4
                  ♡ A 5 2
                  ◇ 6 4
                  ♣ 4 2
```

On the return of the seven of hearts the declarer is helpless. If he ducks, West wins with the ten and knocks out the ace of diamonds, making it impossible for the declarer to score more than one club trick. If South wins the first heart, West wins the first club and gives you two more heart tricks. Either way, South is left wishing that his partner had tried three no trumps.

This defence to four spades would be far from easy to find at the table. However, the analysis gives an insight into the way an expert defender sets about his task. Using a combination of logic and imagination to isolate the only chance, he does not hesitate to back his judgement up to the hilt. That is what good defence is all about.